Object Lessons

Answering kids' toughest questions about God

NEW!
with ideas for use
ANYWHERE!
around the world!

by the Creative
Outreach Team at

kidzana
MINISTRIES
Mukilteo, Washington

Published by   Kidzana Ministries
                      8229 44th Avenue West (Suite G)
                      Mukilteo, WA 98275

Cover design by Bob Horn, eternaldesigngraphics.com.

Written by Sylvia Foth and Annie Crain.

First edition edited by Karin Fleegal, Rod Foth and Kathy Peterson.
Second edition edited by Kimberle Fowle, Sheryl Grunwald, Jan Janofski, Elise Morrison and Bethanie Westbrook.

ISBN 1-930212-06-0

Contents

PART 6: Questions about God & Me

PART 7: Questions about God & Eternity

Preface

Today's kids ask big questions. Although, in this information age, they have a world of facts available at their fingertips, most are not finding satisfactory answers to their pressing questions about God. Many are not hearing the truth about Jesus in terms they can understand. It's no wonder so few are choosing to follow him beyond childhood.

These object lessons were designed to be powerful teaching tools to help you make abstract, complicated Bible truth simple for your students to understand. Each lesson focuses on one main point. For some questions, entire books have been written, trying to explain the Biblical answers. In no way will all your students' questions be satisfied by this one book. These lessons are just a beginning.

We originally wrote this book for a North American audience. However, this release includes "Ideas for Use Anywhere" to help teachers adapt these lessons for use in areas with limited resources, differences in cultural norms, and differences in educational experiences. Even so, some of the lessons will not be suitable in some areas. We've tried to let you know.

Our prayer is that these lessons will not only delight and involve kids, but that they will also help your kids gain a deeper understanding of God, themselves, and Christ's incredible love for them. We hope this book will open up for you the opportunity to dialogue about Christ with your students at a deeper level than ever before. We hope, as a result, that many children will choose to begin – and continue – their relationship with Jesus Christ for a lifetime.

May God give you wisdom and joy as you and your kids face these big questions together!

His for the Kids,

Creative Outreach Team
KIDZANA MINISTRIES

How to Use this Book

This manual contains dozens of kid-tested object lessons for presentation to grade school children (ages 5-12). The lessons are adaptable and may be used in almost any children's setting.

● Opening Bible Fun

Use one object lesson every week to catch your kids' attention at the beginning of a class session. You may choose beforehand which question to address or write several questions on index cards and let students choose the question. In this case, be ready to present any one of the object lessons related to questions that children select.

● Bible Story or Bible Verse Illustration

When teaching Bible stories or Bible verses with tough concepts, use one of these object lessons to help kids gain a deeper understanding. Check out the indexes at the end of the book to find out which demonstrations correspond with different Bible verses and Bible stories.

● Mini-Series on Tough Questions

Choose six or seven questions of most interest to your students, possibly one in each main category. Use one question each week as the theme for a whole lesson. Select one of the Bible verses listed as a memory verse. Do the object demonstration with your kids, then tell one of the Bible stories listed at the end of the lesson. Work together in class on "Something Extra."

Preparing to Teach

● Use these lessons for school-age children

Though younger children may enjoy some of these demonstrations, they are intended for use with children ages 5-12. Younger children are concrete thinkers and may not be able to grasp or correctly understand abstract concepts.

● Read the lessons ahead of time

Take time to read the entire lesson. Look up the scriptures. Pray. Ask God to help you have a clear understanding of the topic before discussing it with children.

● Adjust to local resources

Gather supplies so everything is ready when it is time for the lesson to begin. Make adjustments if some items are not available. Look for ways to make the lesson fun and meaningful for children, even if you make substitutions.

● Adapt lessons for your unique class

Children in every classroom, every community, every culture and every nation are unique. As you prepare to teach the lesson, think about how your children will respond. What additional questions will they have? What other information will they need to know about the topic? Make adjustments as necessary so the lessons are life-changing for your students.

● Include students in discussion

Questions in the lesson are found in **bold** letters. These are suggested to help you begin a dialogue with your students about the topic. Carefully listen to children as they share their thoughts. Give many students a chance to speak. Enjoy helping them participate with the lesson.

Are you ready? Here we go ...

PART 1

Questions about God

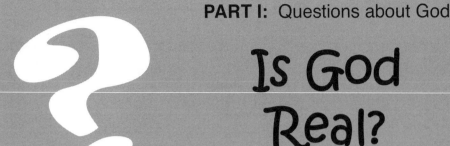

Is God Real?

Materials

❑ picture books, photos or drawings of planets, stars, outer space

The Answer

Yes! God is definitely real. He has revealed himself to all people, since the beginning of time, through his creation.

Bible Proof

●●● **ROMANS 1:20** - For since the creation of the world God's invisible qualities – his eternal power and divine nature – have been clearly seen, being understood from what has been made, so that men are without excuse.

●●● **PSALM 19:1-3** - The heavens declare the glory of God; the skies proclaim the work of his hands. Day after day they pour forth speech; night after night they display knowledge. There is no speech or language where their voice is not heard.

Lesson Aim

To discover that we can know God is real by studying God's creations, like the universe.

Before you teach ...

Many children do not believe God is real because they do not have the luxury of seeing him with their own eyes. Nevertheless, kids can know God is real without even picking up a Bible. All people can look at the earth and sky and see evidence of God's existence. The things God created, like the planets, tell us much about God in terms all people can understand. God did not keep himself a secret. We can know he is real!

TO DO LIST:

❑ Find pictures of planets, stars, galaxies, the solar system, etc. Check with a library or the Internet. Pictures should show how big, orderly, interesting and beautiful space is.

❑ Pray!

 # THE LESSON

Introduction: Begin your lesson by asking students whether they think God is real. **What proof do we have that God is or is not real?** Many students may share that they know God is real because the Bible tells them or because their prayers were answered. **But what about the people who have no Bible or who don't know about prayer? Can they know God is real? How?**

Demonstration: Divide students into pairs and invite them to study the photographs of the universe. Ask each pair to report at least one truth people might learn about God by studying space, the sky or stars.

Discussion: **What might the universe teach us about God?** Help your students to discover and discuss these truths:
- Space is **big** – God must be **big.**
- Space is **orderly** – the sun rises every day. Planets do not bump into each other or drop out of orbit. God must be **orderly.**
- Space shows awesome **power** - the sun burns so hot that it heats our entire planet from millions of miles away. It is powerful! God must be **powerful**, also.
- Space is **interesting and beautiful** – Saturn's rings, sunshine, stars … are all **beautiful and interesting.** God must be, too!

Application: Invite a student to read Romans 1:20 or Psalm 19:1-3. **What difference does it make to kids (and all people) that they can know God is real, even without reading the Bible?** We can have more confidence that God is real and that the Bible is real because both give us evidence that God exists. We can also be happy in knowing how much God loves ALL the people of the world. He made it obvious for every person, in every generation, in every country to know him and serve him.

Ideas for Use Anywhere

- ❑ In areas without access to books, pictures or the Internet, suggest going outdoors to look at the real thing: sun, sky, etc.

- ❑ In developing areas children may not have learned about space or science. Focus on what they know about – the moon, sun, stars.

Something Extra: Invite students to spend a night this week watching the night sky with their families. Ask them to make a few observations and bring them to share next time. **Did they learn anything about God from watching the sky?**

BIBLE STORY IDEA
WISE MEN FOLLOW THE STAR (Matthew 2:1-12)
The wise men saw the star. They followed it and found Jesus. They learned that he came from God. They learned God is real.

How smart is God?

Materials

- ❑ a tape measure
- ❑ several non-fiction books (encyclopedias, dictionaries, textbooks, etc.)

The Answer

God's understanding has no limit. Only he knows the contents of every book ever written.

Bible Proof

- ●●●**ISAIAH 40:28 -** Do you not know? Have you not heard? The Lord is the everlasting God, the Creator of all the ends of the earth. He will not grow tired or weary, and his understanding no one can fathom.
- ●●●**1 CORINTHIANS 1:25 -** For the foolishness of God is wiser than man's wisdom, and the weakness of God is stronger than man's strength.

Lesson Aim

To help students discover that, though people may know many things, their knowledge has limits. God, on the other hand, knows all things, and his knowledge cannot be measured.

Before you teach ...

Modern children wonder how much God really knows. Few realize how incredibly wise and smart he is. In this lesson you have the privilege of guiding your students to recognize that God is even smarter than parents, pastors, school teachers or scientists. Why does it make a difference? If God is this smart, his words in the Bible can always be trusted to help and guide your students with any question or problem they have. Wonderful!

TO DO LIST:

- ❑ Gather materials.
- ❑ Pray for your students by name.

 # THE LESSON

Introduction: Ask students to tell you who the smartest person they know is and why. **What has that person taught you that you didn't know before? Where do you think they learned that fact?** Discover that every person has to learn every bit of information they know from someone else.

Demonstration: Ask for a volunteer who thinks he or she knows someone really smart. Instruct the volunteer to hold his arms out in front of himself. Invite other children to each place a book on the volunteer's arms. **Do you think your friend knows everything in these books? Is your friend this smart?** Keep adding books until the student says to stop, or the student can hold no more. Measure how tall the stack of books is. Wow! This friend is smart. **How smart is God? Is he as smart as the student's friend? How tall would God's stack of books measure?** God is smarter than every person on earth. He knows MORE than all the knowledge in all the books. He made it all, so he knows it all. We cannot measure his understanding. *(Invite the volunteer to be seated.)*

Discussion: Read Isaiah 40:28. **How smart does the Bible say God is?** He knows everything. **How does it help us to know that God knows everything?** He can help us with any problem or question we have. **Where can we find God's "smart" words?** In the Bible. God knows even more than what is in the Bible. He knows everything.

Application: **How can we learn more of God's words and wisdom?** Older students can read the Bible on their own. Read one or two verses a day and think about them. If students cannot read, they can ask parents to read to them, and they can learn God's Word in church.

Something Extra: Invite students to read Isaiah 40:12. Challenge them to look in books or on the Internet this week to see if any man has found out the answers to these questions: **How much water is on the earth? How big is the sky? How much do the mountains weigh? How big would a basket have to be to hold all the dust on the earth?** Enjoy discovering that God knows the answers.

Ideas for Use Anywhere

❑ The Internet may not be accessible to all children in all areas. For "Something Extra" invite them to ask a teacher or "smart person" to help them find the answers.

BIBLE STORY IDEAS

SOLOMON RECEIVES WISDOM (1 Kings 3-4:34)
King Solomon was the wisest man who ever lived. His wisdom and knowledge were not his own. They came from God, who is smartest of all.

BOY JESUS AT THE TEMPLE (Luke 2:41-52)
Even at an early age, Jesus surprised wise teachers in the temple. He was so smart, because he had all of God's knowledge in him. He is God.

Who made God?

Materials

- ❑ hula hoop(s), bicycle tire or other large ring
- ❑ an erasable board

The Answer

No one made God. He has always been and will always be.

Bible Proof

● ● ● **PSALM 90:2 -** Before the mountains were born or you brought forth the earth and the world, from everlasting to everlasting you are God.

● ● ● **REVELATION 1:8 -** "I am the Alpha and the Omega," says the Lord God, "who is, and who was, and who is to come, the Almighty."

Lesson Aim

To show that just as a hula hoop has no beginning or end, God has no beginning or end. He has always been and will always be.

Before you teach ...

One of the most common questions kids ask has to do with the origin of God. A student's belief in this area will greatly affect his or her faith. The Bible teaches that God has always been and will always be. He has no beginning or end. This fact can give great security to children. God is Lord over all history. Surely, he can be trusted to help your students with every aspect of their lives from the time they are young until they grow old.

TO DO LIST:

- ❑ Gather materials.
- ❑ Prepare to tell students what you appreciate most about God.

? THE LESSON

Introduction: Begin your lesson by asking students whether they have ever wondered where God came from. **Who made God?** Listen to student answers. Write these on an erasable board, if you wish. Tell students that they can discover the true Bible answer to this question by studying a hula hoop.

Demonstration: Divide students into small "research" groups. Give each a hula hoop. Challenge each group to examine the hoop. Discover several facts about the object. After a few minutes of studying, twirling, touching, and closely examining the hoop, invite students to be seated. Ask each group to report at least one fact they learned about their hula hoop.

Discussion: **In what ways might a hula hoop be like God?** Listen for student answers. **Does the hula hoop have a beginning?** No. **Does it have an end?** No. **Is this like God? Does God have a beginning? Does God have an end?** The Bible teaches that no one created God. He has always been and will always be.

Application: Invite a student who enjoys reading aloud to read Psalm 90:2. **What difference does it make to kids that God has no beginning or end?** He will always be alive to help us. He has always been around to make good plans and cause his will to come true. He is always around to help keep the world from getting out of control.

Something Extra: If God has always been and always will be, your students can be friends with God for a lifetime. Invite kids who have never received Jesus as their Savior to do so and begin a friendship with God today. Challenge those who have already done so to thank God that he will be their friend all their lives – and forever!

Ideas for Use Anywhere

❑ Hula hoops are not available worldwide. Substitute a bicycle tire or other large circle or ring. Instead of the hula hoop activity, a student may try rolling the tire as far as possible.

❑ Be aware that not all children will be able to read aloud comfortably. Adjust.

BIBLE STORY IDEAS

CREATION (Genesis 1)
Long ago, before anyone else lived, God created the heavens and the earth. He did not need to be created, since he already existed. He has always been.

BIRTH OF CHRIST (Matthew 1:18-2:23; Isaiah 7:14, Micah 5:2)
Christ's birth was predicted long ago by God. Only God, who has always been and will always be, could cause so many detailed prophecies to come true over hundreds – even thousands – of years.

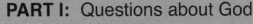

Does God make mistakes?

Materials

❑ a plastic garbage bag, tarp or cloth

❑ a plate or tray

❑ variety of dry foods (crackers, chips, marshmallows, etc.)

The Answer

God never makes mistakes because he is holy, and everything he does is perfect.

Bible Proof

●●● **DEUTERONOMY 32:4 -** He is the Rock, his works are perfect, and all his ways are just. A faithful God who does no wrong, upright and just is he.

●●● **JOB 34:10b & 12 -** Far be it from God to do evil, from the Almighty to do wrong ... It is unthinkable that God would do wrong, that the Almighty would pervert justice.

Lesson Aim

To show that just as food will not stick to a plate, accusations of God doing wrong will not stick to God because he is perfect.

Before you teach ...

Kids begin to learn early that people make mistakes. Friends let them down, teachers get mixed up, and even parents may disappoint them. God is different. He is without sin; therefore he cannot make mistakes. This is why kids can trust him at ALL times in their lives. He never fails.

TO DO LIST:

❑ Gather materials.

❑ Spread the bag or tarp out on the floor before the demonstration. Have paper towels or rags on hand to clean up sticky fingers, if necessary.

❑ Pray for your students.

 THE LESSON

Introduction: Ask your students whose advice they listen to and follow. **Why? Do the people who advise you ever make mistakes?** God gives us instructions he wants us to follow in the Bible. **Should we trust what God says, or does he make mistakes, too?**

Demonstration: Lay the plastic/garbage bag down under the demonstration area. Ask a volunteer to hold the plate up vertically. Then give each student a chance to hit the plate with a piece of the food. **Does the food stick?** No!

Discussion: How is this ceramic plate like God? Read either of the verses listed earlier. **Does God make mistakes?** He is perfect. Just as the foods cannot stick to the plate, so sin cannot stick to God. He is totally without sin. The Bible word for this is "holy." No accusations could stick to Jesus, God's Son, either. People accused him of doing wrong things, but when the facts were checked, no one could find any wrong that Jesus had done. He alone is the only perfect person, without sin. He alone was acceptable to be the sacrifice for our sins. He is holy, holy, holy. He is God.

Application: How does it help us to know that God is perfect? We can trust him at all times. We may make mistakes. Even those who care for us may make mistakes, but God never does. **What do you need God's perfect help with today?** Alone or in small groups, pray to our perfect God about pressing needs. Thank God for being so trustworthy.

Ideas for Use Anywhere

❑ Avoid using food that will be wasted in developing areas of the world. Instead, use dried beans, or other childhood items like hair bands, socks, tissues, etc. that can be dusted off and used again afterwards.

❑ If the group is large, invite only one or two students to demonstrate.

Something Extra: Ask the kids to keep a mental list of mistakes they make this week. Notice which "mistakes" broke God's laws. **Which were sin?** Ask God for forgiveness for these. He cleans our hearts from sin when we ask (1 John 1:9).

BIBLE STORY IDEAS

THE TRIALS OF JESUS (Matthew 26:57-67 and Luke 22:66-23:25) Jesus was accused of doing many wrong things, but none of the accusations "stuck." He was crucified, though he did not deserve it.

THE TEMPTATION OF CHRIST (Matthew 4:1-11) Jesus was tempted, but he never sinned. He did not give in. He is God. This is why he could live a perfect life.

How can God be "in me" and "in heaven" at the same time?

Materials

- ❏ one balloon for each student
- ❏ permanent markers

The Answer

God can be all places at one time, just like air is all around us. But he will not live in our hearts as our Savior unless we invite him to.

Bible Proof

● ● ● **PSALM 139:7-10** - Where can I go from your Spirit? Where can I flee from your presence? If I go up to the heavens, you are there; if I make my bed in the depths, you are there. If I rise on the wings of the dawn, if I settle on the far side of the sea, even there your hand will guide me, your right hand will hold me fast.

● ● ● **REVELATION 3:20** - Here I am! I stand at the door and knock. If anyone hears my voice and opens the door, I will come in and eat with him, and he with me.

Lesson Aim

To show that just as air can totally surround a balloon and also be in it, God can be everywhere – even in heaven – and also be in us, if we have invited him to be part of our lives.

Before you teach ...

Because their bodies can only be in one place at a time, kids have difficulty understanding how God can be in more than one place at a time. But God is far different from us. When Jesus told the disciples he was going to go to heaven to prepare a place for them, he also promised he would send the Holy Spirit, and he would still be with them. What comfort it gives us to know we are not alone. If we believe in him, he is with us and in us, always.

TO DO LIST:

- ❏ Gather materials.
- ❏ If using balloons, check for latex allergies before giving one to each student.
- ❏ Pray for your students.

 THE LESSON

Introduction: **Where is God right now?** Listen for a variety of answers. **Can God be in heaven and in our hearts at the same time? How is this possible?**

Demonstration: Give each student a balloon. Instruct them to place it on the ground. **Is air touching the balloon?** Toss empty balloons in the air and ask the same question. Have them put their balloons anywhere they want in the room, and ask the question. Yes, air is always touching the balloon. Finally, invite them to inflate the balloons. **Where is the air now?** Air is all around it AND inside it. **Did the air go into the balloon all by itself?** No. Someone had to purposefully put it into the balloon. Have the students let the air out of their balloons and put them away until they go home. *(Write names on students' balloons with markers and save them to hand out at the end of class; then kids will not be tempted to play with them during the lesson.)*

Discussion: **How are the balloon and air like God and us? Can God be both in heaven and in you at the same time?** Yes! He is everywhere, surrounding every person in the world, whether they believe in him or not. **How did the air get into the balloon?** Someone purposefully put it in there. **How does Jesus get into our lives?** We must purposefully invite him in. Ask a student to read Revelation 3:20. Jesus will wait outside the imaginary door of our hearts, knocking patiently, until we give him permission to come into our lives. When Jesus is not in us, our lives are empty; but when he comes in, our lives are full!

Application: **Have you asked Jesus to be in you and with you always? Have you "let him in"?** If not, students may pray to receive Jesus as their Savior today. **How does it help us all to know that God is everywhere at once?** We are never alone. He is always near to help us. We can always talk with him.

Ideas for Use Anywhere

❑ If a balloon is not available, use a plastic bag instead.

❑ This demonstration may be done with a single balloon (or bag) in front of the whole group, instead of giving a balloon to each child.

Something Extra: If children each receive balloons, invite them to take these home and show this demonstration to someone who needs to know about Jesus. Invite the friend to open the imaginary door of his or her heart to let Jesus come in to live forever.

BIBLE STORY IDEAS

JESUS PROMISES THE HOLY SPIRIT (John 14) Jesus promised that the Holy Spirit would always be with his disciples.

PARABLE OF THE WEDDING BANQUET (Matthew 22:1-14) Everyone is invited to the "banquet" to enjoy a forever relationship with God. It begins now, on earth, and continues in heaven for eternity.

If God is so powerful, why doesn't he fix all our problems?

Materials

❏ an electronic remote control (and the TV or DVD that it controls, optional)

The Answer

God is powerful enough to fix all the problems on earth, but God has given people the freedom to choose whether to obey him or not. He allows our choices to have natural consequences.

Bible Proof

●●● **JOHN 16:33** - I have told you these things, so that in me you may have peace. In this world you will have trouble. But take heart! I have overcome the world.

●●● **ROMANS 8:28** - And we know that in all things God works for the good of those who love him, who have been called according to his purpose.

Lesson Aim

To show that God does not control people's actions, like he could. People's bad choices often lead to bad consequences (problems).

Before you teach ...

Today, people often question the reality of a loving, powerful God, simply because suffering and trouble exist in the world. If he really cared, wouldn't he fix our problems? God is powerful enough to fix everything, but he loves people enough to let them all make their own choices. He did not make people to be robots. However, he does not leave us to deal with our troubles alone. He gives us the choice to call out to him for help. He will answer!

TO DO LIST:

❏ Gather materials.

❏ Read Bible references and pray about them.

?: THE LESSON

Introduction: **What are some of the problems in our world?** War, pollution, discrimination, hunger, etc. *(Write several down to pray about later.)* **Why doesn't God fix all the problems in the world?** Take some time to listen to the responses (right or wrong). Then invite students to learn the lesson of the remote control.

Demonstration: Show students the remote. **What is this for? How does it work?** *(If a TV or DVD is available, let a student demonstrate how to change a channel or turn the TV on and off.)* Whenever we want to change what we are watching, we simply push a button. The remote gives us the power to control the TV.

Discussion: **How is this remote control like God and us?** God has power over us and every event in the world. **How is the remote NOT like God?** Though God could, he does not push a button and force us to do exactly what he wants us to do. He lets people make their own choices. **Why does God do this?** He loves us. He made us to have a free will. Animals were not made with this same freedom to choose right from wrong. He gives us freedom to choose a relationship with him, or not! **Do people always choose well?** No! They often choose to follow their own way instead of God's. Every choice, like this, has consequences. **Which world problems are caused by people's ungodly choices?** Fighting, discrimination, etc. **What if everyone decided to simply be loving and kind for just one week?** The world would be a totally different place.

Application: **Are you making choices to follow God's way every day? What difference might this make in your life?** Following God's way can help eliminate many bad consequences for us. **Do you have troubles that are not a result of your own bad choices?** God can help us. Read John 16:33. We can pray, asking Jesus for his help with our troubles. He hears and answers our prayers.

Ideas for Use Anywhere

❑ Remote controls are not available everywhere. In this case, skip this lesson.

❑ If a newspaper is not available, tell a story about a big problem.

Something Extra: Invite each student to bring in a newspaper article telling about a big problem somewhere in the world. Pray about these together.

BIBLE STORY IDEAS

THE FALL OF ADAM AND EVE (Genesis 2 & 3)
Adam and Eve chose to disobey God. Their choices resulted in consequences that affected every person ever born on earth.

JOB (Job 1-2, especially Job 1:21-22)
Job, a righteous man, was loved by God, yet God allowed him to suffer for a time. He recognized that God was still in charge and still loved him.

Is God three different gods or just one?

Materials

- ❑ ice
- ❑ a glass of water
- ❑ an electric teapot or steam iron with water
- ❑ concordance (optonal)

The Answer

The Lord God is one, but in three persons: the Father, the Son, and the Holy Spirit.

Bible Proof

● ● ● **DEUTERONOMY 6:4 -** Hear, O Israel: The LORD our God, the LORD is one.

● ● ● **MATTHEW 3:16-17 -** ... Jesus was baptized ... At that moment heaven was opened, and he saw the Spirit of God descending like a dove and lighting on him. And a voice from heaven said, "This is my Son, whom I love; with him I am well pleased."

● ● ● **1 PETER 1:1-2 -** To God's elect ... who have been chosen according to the foreknowledge of God the Father, through the sanctifying work of the Spirit, for obedience to Jesus Christ and sprinkling by his blood: Grace and peace be yours in abundance.

Lesson Aim

To show that just as water is one solution, taking three forms, the Lord God is one God, revealed to us in three forms: Father, Son and Holy Spirit.

Before you teach ...

The subject of the Trinity confuses both adults and kids. How many gods are there? How can he be three, but one, at the same time? God is so complex and difficult for our minds to grasp, yet he has given us ways of understanding himself through nature. Enjoy discovering God "in the water" today.

TO DO LIST:

- ❑ Pour a glass of water.
- ❑ Keep ice in a cooler.
- ❑ Locate the teapot or iron. Find an electrical outlet in which to plug it when ready.

 **THE LESSON**

Introduction: Read Matthew 28:19. **Why does the Bible talk about God the Father, God the Son and God the Holy Spirit? Is there just one God, or are there three?** Invite students to share some of their answers (even if all are incorrect).

Demonstration: Ask one of the students to hold a glass of water. **What's in this glass?** Water. Invite another student look in the ice chest and pick up one of the ice pieces. **What is this? What is ice made from? Is ice a different substance from the water in the glass?** Both are water but in different forms. One is liquid and one is solid. Now, allow the teapot or iron to heat and let off steam. **What is this substance called?** Steam. **What is it made from? Is it different or the same as ice and this glass of water?** It is the same substance but in a different form.

Discussion: **How is the water like God?** God is one God; there will never be another, just as water will always be water. But there are three different forms of God: Father, Son and Holy Spirit … three persons, all one God. **What would the world be like if we didn't have ice or steam but only water? What would the world be like if we didn't have Jesus or the Holy Spirit?** The Trinity helps us to understand more about how wonderful God is.

Application: **How does it help you to know that there is just one God but with three different forms? How is it good to know that God the Father loves us? What does it do for you to have Jesus' example of how to live a loving, perfect life? How does the Holy Spirit, who is in you and with you always, help your life every day?** Thank God for describing himself as three persons, allowing us to have a better understanding of how awesome and wonderful he is.

Ideas for Use Anywhere

❑ In some teaching situations, ice and steam may not be available. Simply show a cup of water, and imagine the other forms of water.

❑ Allow time for students to discuss their answers to the many questions.

Something Extra: Work together in small groups. Give one group a paper headed "Father," another group the heading "Jesus," and a third "The Holy Spirit." Have each group write down attributes for the name of God they have listed. Use the concordance, if possible. **How does the Bible describe each?**

BIBLE STORY IDEAS

THE BAPTISM OF JESUS (Matthew 3:13-17)
At Jesus' baptism, he heard the voice of God the Father and saw the Spirit descending on him like a dove. All were there: one God.

THE GREAT COMMISSION (Matthew 28:16-20)
Jesus sent his disciples out to tell everyone in the world about him, baptizing them in the name of the Father, the Son and the Holy Spirit.

PART 2

Questions about God and Creation

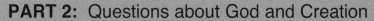

Wasn't the world created by accident?

Materials

☐ an old watch, clock, radio or motor, disassembled (or parts to look like they belong to one of these creations)

The Answer

No! The earth could not have been created as the result of an accidental explosion. It was planned, crafted and created by God.

Bible Proof

●●● **GENESIS 1:1 -** In the beginning God created the heavens and the earth.

●●● **PSALM 102:25 -** In the beginning you laid the foundations of the earth, and the heavens are the work of your hands.

Lesson Aim

To show that just as a clock cannot be assembled by shaking its parts together in a bag, the earth could not come together perfectly by chance.

Before you teach ...

If your students attend public school – and even if they do not – they will be challenged by the prevailing scientific belief that the world was created by an accidental "big bang." Today's lesson will help kids to see that a random explosion simply could not have resulted in the creation of our incredibly perfect earth. God designed and planned it all.

TO DO LIST:

☐ Locate an old watch, clock, radio or motor. Take the pieces apart and place in a clear plastic bag; or simply gather metal screws, springs, and parts that might look as if they belong to this item, disassembled.

? THE LESSON

Introduction: Begin the lesson by asking students, **"How do many scientists believe the world was formed?"** By the "big bang". They think it came together as the result of an unplanned explosion in space. **What does the Bible say? Can the Bible's version of creation really be true?**

Demonstration: Show the bag to your students. If a tray is available, dump the contents out for all students to see. Notice all the pieces. Realize that these are the parts to a clock (or other creation of technology). Place the pieces in the bag. Ask your students if they think the pieces can be put together to work again. Shake the bag. Give everyone in the class — or several volunteers — a chance to shake the bag. Check inside. **Is the item assembled? Is it even partly together?** No!

Discussion: Can the clock ever come together by shaking? Why not? Because a clock must be carefully assembled by someone who is trained to do it properly. He must know how the pieces are designed and then put them together in exactly the right way. **In what way is this like the creation of the universe?** It is so complicated, perfect, and intricate, that it could not possibly come together as the result of an unplanned explosion. The earth shows signs of being carefully designed and crafted to work together in perfect order, even better than a clock.

Application: Invite a student reader to read Psalm 102:25. **What does the Bible teach about the creation of the world? Did it come together by accident? What difference does this make to kids?** We can personally talk to the One who made the universe and us. If he has power to create this beautiful, perfect planet home for us, he can certainly help us with other problems we might have.

Something Extra: Challenge your students to look for complicated things in nature during the coming week. Study a plant. Study their own hand. Study a bug or other creature. **Could these have come about by accident?** Thank God for designing such an incredible world.

Ideas for Use Anywhere

❑ Another possibility: Use a shoe. Remove laces. See if the shoe laces and ties itself by shaking it in a bag.

❑ Some students may not be familiar with "big bang" or science concepts.

BIBLE STORY IDEA

CREATION (Genesis 1; Psalm 104)
In the beginning God created the earth. Each day of creation he added another significant aspect to our world. Each was planned and designed to work together perfectly. This did not happen by accident.

Couldn't an explosion have created the earth?

Materials

- ❑ a can or bottle of soda pop
- ❑ tarp, towels or garbage bags

The Answer

No. Explosions usually destroy. Only God's explosive power could create something as perfect as our earth.

Bible Proof

●●● **COLOSSIANS 1:16-17 -** For by him all things were created … He is before all things, and in him all things hold together.

●●● **JEREMIAH 32:17 -** Ah, Sovereign Lord, you have made the heavens and the earth by your great power and outstretched arm. Nothing is too hard for you.

Lesson Aim

To show that just as the power released from a shaken soda can creates a mess, other kinds of random power in nature are also destructive. God's power is huge, but perfectly creative.

Before you teach …

Scientists are creating and unleashing more and more of nature's power all the time. Kids want to know whether some natural source of power besides God could have created the earth. The laws of nature teach us that earth's elements are moving from a state of order to disorder. It is impossible for things to come together logically through a random explosion. Only God's power could result in the creation of our perfect earth.

TO DO LIST:

- ❑ Cover the demonstration area with tarps, garbage bags or towels; or, better yet, perform this demonstration outdoors to avoid a mess.

- ❑ Pray!

20

? THE LESSON

Introduction: Ask your students to describe the most incredible display of power they have ever seen (a building demolition, a rocket launch, explosion, earthquake, tornado, etc.). **Did the power ultimately bring about destruction, or did it bring something together?** Large doses of random power destroy. **If this is true, why do many scientists believe that the earth began as the result of a "big bang" explosion? Could it really have happened that way?**

Demonstration: Invite your students to try an experiment to see what can be created from a little power and a little soda pop. Let each kid shake the unopened can or bottle. **What will happen when we open this soda?** Open it and "unleash the power." The soda should fizz and spray all over.

Discussion: **What did our explosion create?** A mess. **Do explosions usually create or destroy?** Destroy. **How is this different from God's power?** God's power is big and explosive, but also creative and controlled. When his power is at work, he creates. **Could the earth have been created by a big burst of random power?** Many scientists believe that the earth began as the result of a "big bang." They believe this powerful explosion set forces into motion that created our beautiful, orderly, and perfect-working universe. This earth is complicated, complex, and works together in the universe like a perfectly tuned clock or cell phone. **Could this happen by accident?** No.

Application: Read Jeremiah 32:17. God made the heavens and the earth. This was not too hard for him at all. God made order out of chaos in creation. **What is out of order in your life? What do you need God to help with? Does he have power to help? How do we know?** If he has the power to create the earth, he also has power to help with any problem. He loves to help his people, including kids.

Ideas for Use Anywhere

☐ If Coca Cola® or soda is not available, use a cup with vinegar. Drop a spoonful of baking soda in the glass and watch it foam and fizz.

☐ Avoid wasting a bottle of soda in areas where food is scarce.

Something Extra: Invite students to ask five friends or teachers to tell them how they believe the earth came to be. Report back next time. **How many believe God created the earth? How many believe it was a result of an unplanned explosion?** Pray for a chance to talk to those who do not believe in God's creative power.

BIBLE STORY IDEA
CREATION (Genesis 1)
God created the heavens and the earth. He simply spoke the words, and they came to be. He is awesome!

How are God's creations different from people's creations?

Materials

❑ a lump of playing dough for each pair of students (if possible)

The Answer

People can create things only from what God has already given us. Only God can make something out of nothing. Only God can create life.

Bible Proof

●●●**GENESIS 2:7 -** The Lord God formed the man from the dust of the ground and breathed into his nostrils the breath of life, and the man became a living being.

●●●**HEBREWS 11:3 -** By faith we understand that the universe was formed at God's command, so that what is seen was not made out of what was visible.

Lesson Aim

To show that just as kids cannot create a real person out of a lump of playing dough, no person can create life. Only God can do this.

Before you teach ...

Modern kids are constantly challenged to be creative. They come to believe that with enough imagination, teamwork and technology, people can accomplish anything. And many impressive inventions testify to this truth. Nevertheless, as wonderful as all of man's creations are, they pale compared to God's. Only God can create something out of nothing. Only he can breathe life into people. He is so much greater than anything people can possibly invent themselves.

TO DO LIST:

❑ Get enough playing dough for each pair of students to have a lump about the size of their fist. Before class, divide the dough and place in small clear plastic zipper bags or in a covered container.

❑ Pray!

 THE LESSON

Introduction: **What are some of your favorite inventions?** Think about toys, foods, games, vehicles, etc. **How are God's creations different from man's creations?** Invite students to participate in a demonstration to help them understand the difference.

Demonstration: Let each student choose a partner. Give each pair a lump of playing dough. Invite one partner to take the first turn, trying to form the dough into the shape of his or her partner. After several minutes, check their work. Enjoy the funny results. Then trade roles, giving the next partner a turn to shape the dough. **How does it look?** *(If group is large, two students may do this for the whole class.)*

Discussion: **Did you make real people? Why not? Is it easy to even copy another person's shape with the playing dough?** Sculptors spend years and years learning to shape clay into perfect human replicas. **Can they make real people, given more time?** No. Their creations will simply be art. Scientists have learned to clone different animals and even hybrid two different types of vegetables to make a new kind. **Have they actually created life?** No, they used cells of living things that God had already made. Only God can make something out of nothing. He alone is the Giver of Life.

Application: **Who deserves the credit when you make something out of the things God has already created?** God does. Make a list of things kids enjoy playing with that scientists, engineers or artists have made. Next, list the ingredients in these items that were created by God. Thank God for everything he created, including chemicals, fuel to run machinery, people's imagination, etc.

Ideas for Use Anywhere

❑ Playing dough may not be available. Substitute mud or clay. *(Or visit www.kidzana.org for a simple playdough recipe.)*

❑ In developing areas, students will not have discussed science concepts such as "hybrids". Adapt by referring to locally known inventions.

Something Extra: Next time your students visit the grocery store, challenge them to look for a new invention scientists have "created" for us to enjoy. **Who created the ingredients these were developed from?** Thank God.

BIBLE STORY IDEAS

THE GOLDEN CALF (Exodus 32)
While Moses was on Mount Sinai, the people created a calf out of gold. They worshipped it as their "god". The calf could do nothing. It was only gold, a natural element created by God.

JESUS FEEDS 5000 (John 6:1-13)
Jesus multiplied food to feed a crowd of thousands. Can people do this?

Why did God make yucky things?

Materials

- ❑ a cookie for each student (home-baked, if possible)
- ❑ baking soda (or flour)
- ❑ erasable board

The Answer

God made everything good. He made it to work together perfectly. Some of the good "ingredients" God needed for this world seem "yucky", by themselves, to people.

Bible Proof

●●●**GENESIS 1:31a -** God saw all that he had made, and it was very good.

●●●**ROMANS 8:28 -** And we know that in all things God works for the good of those who love him, who have been called according to his purpose.

Lesson Aim

To show that just as baking soda tastes yucky (but is very useful), other items in creation that seem yucky have a role to play in God's perfectly good creation.

Before you teach ...

Bugs. Have you ever seen one? Many kids, when seeing them for the first time, turn up their noses with disgust. How could God make something so unpleasant? The question comes up with many other created things: bugs, mud, rain, dirt, and more. In this lesson, your kids can learn that all these ingredients were needed to be part of the perfectly good world God made for us.

TO DO LIST:

- ❑ Gather materials needed. (Keep the cookies well hidden.)
- ❑ Place baking soda in a small bowl.
- ❑ Pray for your students to understand!

? THE LESSON

Introduction: Begin the lesson by asking students to name some yucky things they have seen in creation. Record several answers. Next, invite a student to read Genesis 1:31a. **Do you think God really created some of these strange things? Did God make a mistake when he made them?**

Demonstration: Get out the baking soda and have each child taste a small pinch. God not only created living things, but substances that are "yucky," too. **Would anyone like to have a scoop of this for dinner tonight? Do you like the taste of it? Why would God bother making such a substance?** If we mixed this with eggs, salt, butter, sugar, flour and vanilla, we could bake cookies. **What would happen if we didn't have baking soda?** The cookies would be flat and hard. They would not taste nearly as good. **Now what do you think of baking soda?**

Discussion: **How is this baking soda like other "yucky" things that God created?** *(Refer to the list recorded during the introduction.)* Again, read Genesis 1:31. God made everything good. EVERYTHING. Even the things that seem yucky have a part in making this world an awesome place for people to live. If there were no bugs, plants might not be pollinated. If there were no chemicals, we might not have the ingredients for air, and we would die. If there were no wind or storms, seeds might not grow in new places. Everything God created belongs.

Application: **Do you think some creatures are too ugly? Why might this creature be important in God's creation? How does it fit within a system in nature?** Thank God for all these things. Thank him for making it all good.

Ideas for Use Anywhere

❑ The word "yucky" will not translate well. Substitute "ugly", "unpleasant" or another synonym.

❑ In many parts of the world, cookies are not common. Substitute a more basic food with one unpleasant tasting ingredient (rice with spices, or sauce with onions).

Something Extra: Challenge your students to find one odd or unusual thing God created and bring it to class next time. **How might this be an important part of God's creation?**

BIBLE STORY IDEAS

PAUL & THE POISONOUS SNAKE (Acts 28:1-10)
God used a poisonous snake to teach unbelievers a lesson about his power.

LOOK AT THE ANTS (Proverbs 6:6-8)
God made ants. Even insects have a part in creation. Ants can even help teach us lessons God wants us to learn.

Aren't people and animals mostly the same?

The Answer

No! People were created in God's own image. Animals were not. Even better, people are created with a soul so they can have a personal relationship with God.

Bible Proof

●●●**1 CORINTHIANS 15:39 -** All flesh is not the same: Men have one kind of flesh, animals have another, birds another and fish another.

●●●**GENESIS 1:26 & 27 -** Then God said, "Let us make man in our image, in our likeness, and let them rule over the fish … birds … livestock … all the earth, and over all the creatures … So God created man in his own image, in the image of God he created him; male and female he created them.

Lesson Aim

To show that though animals and people may have some similar "pieces," animals were not created with the most important piece necessary for knowing God: a soul.

Before you teach ...

Modern kids are taught the value of animals, sometimes to the point of exceeding the worth of human life. Kids need to know there is a difference. We were not created equal. Though God loves and cares for all the creatures he created, his greatest love is for people. First, we are created in his image. But even more, we were created with the unique capacity for having a personal relationship with God through Christ. Animals were not made for the same purpose.

TO DO LIST:

❑ Locate a good puzzle. Take one piece out and hide it somewhere in your classroom.

❑ Pray!

❓ THE LESSON

Introduction: Ask the following questions and listen for your students' answers. **Are people and animals different? Who thinks we are both created mostly the same? Why do you think so? Who thinks we are created differently? Why do you think so? What makes people ... people, and animals ... animals?**

Demonstration: Invite students to work with you on a demonstration to discover one difference between people and animals. Challenge students to quickly put the jigsaw puzzle together. **What do they discover?** A piece is missing. Let the students know that the piece is hidden somewhere in the class. Invite the kids to look for it. Celebrate when it is found.

Discussion: Teach that people are like the puzzle. They are made of many complicated and wonderful parts. Some parts, like bones, muscles, eyeballs, stomachs, etc., seem the same as animals. But animals are missing one important piece: a soul. This piece gives humans the ability to have a personal relationship with God. This part of people makes them unique from animals. Some people have not recognized this piece that needs a personal relationship with Jesus Christ to be full and complete. Without him, we experience less than what God created us to be. Though he cares for all creatures, God did not send Jesus to save them from their sin. They do not choose sin. They do not choose God. They simply do what God gave them instincts to do.

Application: **Have you asked Jesus to fill that important place in your heart?** Now is a good time to ask. God celebrates when we come to know him, just as we celebrated when we finished the puzzle. Our lives were made to know him.

Ideas for Use Anywhere

❑ Jigsaw puzzles are not available everywhere. If possible, create puzzle pieces by cutting a paper into 20 parts. Or use a cell phone and remove the battery.

❑ Science concepts such as "instincts" or knowledge about mammals may be limited in developing areas.

Something Extra: Invite students to spend some time with an animal this week. **How is the animal similar to themselves? How is the animal different? What is wonderful about the animal? Can the creature ever know Jesus?**

BIBLE STORY IDEAS

DO NOT WORRY (Matthew 6:25-35)
God clothes the lilies of the field and notices when a sparrow dies, but he cares even more for his people and provides for their needs.

ADAM NAMES THE ANIMALS (Genesis 2)
Adam was created to rule the earth. He even named animals. Animals were not made to rule.

How hard was it for God to create the earth?

Materials

❑ Legos ® or simple building blocks

The Answer

God's ways are beyond anything man can imagine. He created the heavens and the earth with simple commands from his mouth.

Bible Proof

●●● **PSALM 148:4 & 5b -** Praise him, you highest heavens and you waters above the skies … for he commanded and they were created.

●●● **HEBREWS 11:3 -** By faith we understand that the universe was formed at God's command, so that what is seen was not made out of what was visible.

Lesson Aim

To show that though it would be impossible for man to create a master project without using his hands, God can do it with a simple command.

Before you teach ...

Today's society has accomplished much. Engineers invent new wonders at incredible speed. Kids love new computer games, computer toys and more. In this age of high technology, kids may have difficulty recognizing God's creative power as being more impressive than that of a computer engineer. This lesson teaches your students how incredibly far above man's ways are God's ways. Not only did he create this world out of nothing; he also simply spoke it all into being. Wow.

TO DO LIST:

❑ Gather materials.

❑ Welcome your students by name when you see them next.

 THE LESSON

Introduction: Scientists are very smart these days. **What are some of the new things scientists have made that you think are wonderful? Do you think scientists could have created the world just as easily as God did?**

Demonstration: Ask for one student volunteer who likes science – one who might like to become an engineer later in life. Invite the volunteer to create a perfectly square house with the building toy pieces. Ready, set, WAIT! Give the student one more instruction. The student may not touch the pieces with any part of his or her body. Now, invite the student to begin. Watch expectantly as he or she squirms. **Is it hard to make a square house from these pieces? Why is our volunteer having trouble?** Finally, allow the student to use his or her hands and quickly build the house. Thank the volunteer and ask him or her to be seated.

Discussion: **Why was this assignment impossible?** The volunteer had to create something without using his or her hands. Ask a student to read Hebrews 11:3. The Bible tells us that God created the earth and the universe by a simple command. He told it to become, and it did. People cannot do this, no matter how great at science, or how many years they have studied at a university. **Why?** People are not God. **How did the things God made with no hands turn out? Were they poorly made because he did it too fast?** No! God made wonderful, incredible, perfect things! He is amazing!

Application: God's help is greater than man's. He made everything (even you), so he knows how to help in every situation. **In what way do you need God's help today?** Pray together, asking for God's creative and awesome power to meet any needs. Also, thank him for making us and making this incredible world for us to live in.

Ideas for Use Anywhere

❏ Legos® are not available in many areas. Substitute blocks or bricks to create a tower.

❏ Students might not have access to the library or books. Suggest another creation a child could go home and make on their own.

Something Extra: Invite students to check out a book of experiments from the library and try one out. **What did this experiment teach you about things God created? Could you do this without your hands?** Thank God for his power.

BIBLE STORY IDEAS

SOLOMON BUILDS A TEMPLE (1 Kings 6)
Solomon built a great temple for God. It took eleven years to build, using thousands of people. God created the earth with a few words in six days.

JESUS CALMS THE STORM (Mark 4:35-41)
With a few words, Jesus calms a raging storm.

PART 3

Questions about God and the Bible

Is the Bible really true?

Materials

❑ five dice

❑ a newspaper article mentioning Israel or Palestine (optional)

The Answer

Yes! The Bible really is true. One proof is that promises in the Bible, made thousands of years in advance, have come true with great accuracy.

Bible Proof

●●●**PSALM 33:4 -** For the word of the Lord is right and true; he is faithful in all he does.
●●●**JOHN 19:36a -** These things happened so that the scripture would be fulfilled.
●●●**2 PETER 1:20-21 -** Above all, you must understand that no prophecy of Scripture came about by the prophet's own interpretation. For prophecy never had its origin in the will of man, but men spoke from God as they were carried along by the Holy Spirit.

Lesson Aim

To discover how difficult it is to make accurate predictions, then examine several Bible predictions to see how God caused them to come true.

Before you teach ...

Modern children are thinking children. Though this can be intimidating to adults, it also works for our children's benefit. They will not believe something just because someone tells them. They need proof for almost everything. This impacts children in church, where they need proof, for example, that the Bible is real. In this lesson, they will learn how God's promises, kept over hundreds and even thousands of years, prove that the Bible is God's true Word.

TO DO LIST:

❑ Gather materials.

❑ Locate an article about Israel or Palestine in a newspaper.

? THE LESSON

Introduction: Begin by discussing answers to the following questions with your students. **Can we believe everything people tell us? How do we know what is true? Are movies true? Are commercials? How about the words in the Bible? Are they true? How do we know?** Invite students to discover some proof with you, today, using a bunch of dice.

Demonstration: Give the students a chance to toss all five dice at once. Before each turn, students must tell the others which numbers they predict will be showing on the dice. After several have taken a turn, discuss the results: **Did anyone guess all numbers correctly? Can anyone do this accurately all the time? Is it easy to predict the future? Do we even know what will happen this week?**

Discussion: Look up the following Bible predictions. Discuss whether these things came true or not.
1) The family of Abraham (also known as Israel) would become a great nation. Read Genesis 35:11, then look in the newspaper for Israel or show a current map. **How long have Israel and the Jewish people been around?**
2) A Messiah would be born in Bethlehem. Read Micah 5:2, then Luke 2:11.
3) Jesus will be great. Read Luke 1:31,32. **Is Jesus famous?**
4) Jesus predicted he would die and rise again. Read Luke 18:31-33, then read 1 Corinthians 15:3-8.

Hundreds of years passed between the time the predictions were given and when they came true. **Could the people who wrote the predictions have caused them to happen?** No, they were already dead! **Who could cause this to happen? How does this help us know the Bible is true?** Men wrote the Bible, recording the words God gave them. The predictions came true. God did it. His words are true.

Ideas for Use Anywhere

❑ If dice are not available or acceptable in certain church settings, number 20 slips of paper 1-20. A child guesses a number, then tries to pull that number from the stack.

❑ Be sensitive to strong attitudes toward Israel worldwide. Be willing to affirm God's love for all of Abraham's descendants.

Application: **Do you believe the Bible is true? If so, what will you do about it?** Read it, learn it, obey what it says. The Bible gives us God's guidelines for living life in the best way possible.

Something Extra: Invite kids to read God's Word on their own in the coming week. Read one or two verses. Think about why it is important.

BIBLE STORY IDEA

ISAAC IS PROMISED TO ABRAHAM (Genesis 15:1-6; 18:9-15; 21:1-7) God promised to give Abraham a son. It was impossible, because Abraham and Sarah were very old. God caused it to happen.

Why is the Bible such a big deal?

Materials

- ❑ peanut butter, jelly or jam, bread
- ❑ butter knife and a plate
- ❑ covering for work area

The Answer

The Bible contains God's guidelines for the best life. Our lives turn out messy when we do not follow his directions.

Bible Proof

●●●**PSALM 119:105 -** Your word is a lamp to my feet and a light for my path.

●●●**PSALM 103:17 & 18 -** But from everlasting to everlasting the Lord's love is with those who fear him, and his righteousness with their children's children – with those who keep his covenant and remember to obey his precepts.

Lesson Aim

To show that just as things turn out messy when we do not follow the directions for making a sandwich, life turns out messy when people do not follow God's directions in the Bible.

Before you teach ...

Though the Bible may be true, kids do not always see the value of following its rules. God wants us to follow his guidelines so we can have the best life possible. Statistics show that people who follow God's instructions day after day are less likely to end up in the hospital, to commit suicide or to get divorced, to name a few. In this lesson, kids will learn that following God's Word can help their lives be great!

TO DO LIST:

- ❑ Gather materials.
- ❑ Cover the demonstration area with a towel, plastic or newspaper for easy cleanup.
- ❑ Pray!

 # THE LESSON

Introduction: Ask your students if they like rules. **Which rules are easy to follow? Which rules are hard to follow? Why is the Bible such a big deal to God?** It contains his guidelines for living life in the best possible way. The following demonstration will help your kids understand this better.

Demonstration: Tell your students that you are really hungry, but you forgot your instructions for making a peanut butter and jelly sandwich. **Can they help by telling you how to make it?** Do exactly the opposite of what they tell you to do. When they tell you to spread peanut butter on bread, drop jam on the plate. When they tell you to put the pieces of bread together, put the sticky sides out. **What went wrong? Why didn't this sandwich come together right?** Because the teacher did not follow the directions.

Discussion: **What kinds of instruction does God give us in the Bible?** God gives us commands to obey, promises to believe in, and principles to help us understand life. **What happens if we do not do things the way he tells us?** If we refuse to follow God's instructions, we can make an even bigger mess out of our lives than this sandwich mess. **Why does God give us rules?** He did not give them to be mean; he gives these as instructions for the best life possible. **Why is the Bible such a big deal?** It keeps us out of "messes" and teaches us how to live.

Application: **Can kids really obey God's Word? Are there too many rules?** Some kids may think so. But Jesus helped people to see that obeying God's way came down to simple things: "Love God" and "Love your neighbor as yourself." (Matthew 22:37-39).

Something Extra: Invite students to find the Ten Commandments in Exodus 20. Condense them into simple phrases, writing one phrase on each paper. Then, work together to divide the commandments into two groups: those relating to "Loving God" and those that have to do with "Loving Your Neighbor."

Ideas for Use Anywhere

❑ Peanut butter and jelly are not eaten worldwide. This same demonstration can be done with a child telling an adult how to put on a jacket.

❑ If using peanut butter or food, avoid wasting the food after the demonstration is over.

BIBLE STORY IDEAS

ACHAN'S SINS/BATTLE OF AI (Joshua 7:1-12) Because Achan disobeyed God's instructions, people died needlessly in battle.

THE TWELVE SPIES (Numbers 13 & 14) Ten spies did not have faith to face the giants. They chose not to obey. It cost them 40 years in the wilderness. What a mess!

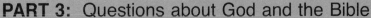

Is the Bible really different from other books?

Materials

- ❑ a concrete or stone brick
- ❑ a gelatin brick
- ❑ cookie sheets or trays
- ❑ towels

The Answer

Yes! The Bible is God's Word. It is totally unique. No other book is as reliable.

Bible Proof

●●● **PSALM 119:89 -** Your word, O Lord, is eternal; it stands firm in the heavens.

●●● **2 TIMOTHY 3:16 -** All scripture is God-breathed and is useful for teaching, rebuking, correcting and training in righteousness.

Lesson Aim

To show that God's words and advice in the Bible are totally reliable, whereas other people's words and advice may not prove reliable over time.

Before you teach ...

Often, kids do not realize that the advice in the Bible is different from other advice about life and getting along. This demonstration will help them to recognize that the Bible is far more reliable a guide for their life than the words of any other book, person or authority. Though some are good, these others will not prove reliable over time. Enjoy strengthening your students' faith in the Word of God today.

TO DO LIST:

- ❑ Gather materials.
- ❑ Make the brick of gelatin, chilling a double strength batch of gelatin in a small loaf pan. Unmold just before class. Keep covered on two separate trays.
- ❑ Pray!

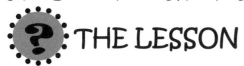 # THE LESSON

Introduction: Announce that you need a volunteer to help you with an experiment. Set the covered trays on the floor (one with a stone brick, one with a gelatin or soft brick). Ask for one volunteer. The student must be willing to take off shoes and socks. Use an adult volunteer if class members are too young.

Demonstration: Invite the volunteer to take off both socks and shoes. Uncover the stone brick. Ask the volunteer to step on it. *(The other brick should not be visible yet.)* **Does the brick hold your weight? Is it strong enough to stand on? Is it sturdy? Will it last?** Yes! It is strong. Next, unveil the gelatin brick. Ask the volunteer to step on this brick. The volunteer stands on the brick, only to find it squishing flat between his or her toes. **Does this brick hold your weight? Is it strong enough to stand on? Is it sturdy? Will it last?** No! It is not strong. It is a mess. Thank the volunteer and ask him or her to be seated. *(Ask an assistant to help the student clean off his or her feet with towels or rags.)*

Discussion: Would you rather build your life on advice that is strong, like the concrete brick, or on advice that might look good, but is not reliable? Most kids will answer that they want to build their lives on something reliable. God's word is like the concrete brick. **How is the Bible different from other people's books?** Other books, though they may contain some good advice, will not always hold true when life's toughest tests come along. The Bible is reliable.

Application: Invite a student reader to read 2 Timothy 3:16. **What difference can God's Word make in a kid's life?** According to this verse, the Bible can teach kids, correct kids, and train them to be righteous. This is the best way to live.

Something Extra: Challenge your students to make a Bible verse "Wrist Wreminder". Cut a strip of fun foam (3/4" X 12"). With a permanent marker, write the first letter of each word in Proverbs 3:5 across the foam strip (like a WWJD bracelet). Tape in place around wrists. Invite students to memorize the verse. Wear the bracelet for a week. **How was this advice different from other advice your students heard during their week?**

Ideas for Use Anywhere

❑ Avoid using this lesson where a mess signals disrespect or waste.

❑ Substitute a loaf of bread, mud or a balloon for the gelatin brick, if needed.

BIBLE STORY IDEAS

SOLOMON ASKS FOR WISDOM (1 Kings 3)
Solomon knew he needed God's wisdom for life's difficulties. He prayed and asked God to help him, and God did.

WISE AND FOOLISH BUILDERS (Matthew 7:24-29)
Jesus taught that our foundation needs to be on hearing and doing what he says. **Where do we find what he says?**

How can such an old book be good for kids?

Materials

- ❏vitamins in a bottle
- ❏Bibles

The Answer

God's book, though written thousands of years ago, is a book that has perfect advice for people of all ages.

Bible Proof

●●●**HEBREWS 4:12 -** The word of God is living and active. Sharper than any double edged sword, it penetrates ... it judges the thoughts and attitudes of the heart.

●●●**PSALM 119:9 -** How can a young man keep his way pure? By living according to your word.

Lesson Aim

To show that just as vitamins have always been essential ingredients for healthy bodies, the Bible, though written many years ago, has ingredients needed for the spiritual health of all people from the beginning of time until the present day.

Before you teach ...

Kids may think the Bible is old fashioned and the words in it do not apply to them. This is not what God says about his Word. He says his Word is essential to us. It is not a book just for the generations in which it was written, but the Word is living and active. The Bible is an essential ingredient to every person's spiritual health, no matter how old or young.

TO DO LIST:

- ❏Optional: prepare a fruit or vegetable snack for your students. Research which vitamins are found in that snack.

 # THE LESSON

Introduction: Discuss with your students how long ago the different parts of the Bible were written. It was written over thousands of years by forty different authors. **Is the Bible outdated now?** Some books that were written just one hundred years ago are already outdated. **Is the Bible any different? How can such an old book be good for kids?**

Demonstration: Show the kids the bottle of vitamins. *(Do NOT give out vitamins in your class. If you wish, you could give students a carrot or piece of fruit and tell them which vitamins are in it.)* **Why are vitamins good for us? How do they help us?** They have ingredients that our bodies need to stay healthy. **What happens to our bodies if we don't get the right vitamins?** Our bodies become unhealthy. They do not work as well as they were designed to work. **Did Noah also need vitamins, from his food, for a healthy body? Did King David? Your mom or dad?** Vitamins are needed by people of all ages to keep their bodies healthy.

Discussion: How is the Bible like vitamins? The ingredients in the Bible are more important to our spiritual health than vitamins are to our physical bodies. All people need vitamins to stay healthy. All people need the Bible to be spiritually healthy. Read Hebrews 4:12. **How is God's Word good for us?** It is living and active. This means it will make a difference in the lives of every generation, not just the people of Bible times. **What happens if we do not get the vitamins we need?** We may become sick. **What happens when we ignore God's Word?** We miss out on the important truth about Jesus and may spiritually die without him as our Savior. We miss God's best for our lives. **Was this true in Bible times, too?**

Application: Have you received Jesus? This is the most important ingredient for eternal spiritual health. Kids can pray today to receive Christ. **How often do people take vitamins?** Daily. **How often do we need God's Word?** Every day, just like vitamins. **How will you "take in" God's Word ("Vitamin W") this week?**

Ideas for Use Anywhere

❑ Vitamin supplements are not used worldwide. Use fruits or vegetables and name beneficial vitamins in each: bananas, carrots, cabbage, tomatoes, etc.

❑ "Vitamin W" will not translate well. Avoid it.

Something Extra: Invite students to read Psalm 19:7-11. List benefits of God's Word. **How are these better than the benefits of vitamins?**

BIBLE STORY IDEAS

JOSIAH FINDS THE BOOK OF LAW (2 Kings 22)
Josiah and the people found God's Word. They read it and obeyed.

YOUNG DAVID (I Samuel 16)
David's heart was pure from a young age. God chose him to be king. How did he keep his way pure? Read Psalm 119:9.

Won't the Bible become extinct soon?

Materials

- ❑ a trick candle
- ❑ matches
- ❑ a cup of water

The Answer

The Word of God will never be extinct. God has kept his Word safe generation after generation. It will last forever.

Bible Proof

●●●**MATTHEW 24:35 -** Heaven and earth will pass away, but my words will never pass away.

●●●**ISAIAH 40:8** - The grass withers and the flowers fall, but the word of our God stands forever.

Lesson Aim

To show that just as a trick candle's flame cannot be extinguished, God's Word in the Bible can never be destroyed.

Before you teach ...

Life changes at such an alarming rate. Knowledge increases rapidly. What was "in" last year is outdated this year. Children growing up in this fast-paced world need today's lesson. Though written hundreds and thousands of years ago, the Bible is still applicable to today. In fact, it is still a best-seller. So? Why will kids care? Because, in this world of rapid change, God's Word is something secure and reliable they can trust in for a lifetime and beyond.

TO DO LIST:

❑ Bring something to support the candle (muffin, lump of playing dough, candlestick).

❑ Be sure a cup of water is handy to extinguish the flame after the demonstration.

❑ Pray!

 THE LESSON

Introduction: Invite students to name books they enjoy reading. **How long ago was the book written? How long will people love this book? Will people be reading it in 100 years or 1000 years? How about the Bible? Will it become extinct soon?** Since the Bible was written so long ago, some kids – and adults – think the Bible is outdated. But this is not true. This demonstration will help us learn the truth about the Bible.

Demonstration: Light the candle and ask two kids to come up and blow it out. After they blow it out, invite them to sit down. Act like the demonstration is over. Be surprised when the candle flames again. Ask another pair to come blow out the candle. Maybe they will do a better job than the first group. **What's wrong? Why can't they blow the candle out either?** It is a trick candle. It is not ordinary.

Discussion: **Do all candles keep flaming again?** No, they do not come back to flame again. **How was our candle different?** It could not be extinguished. **How is this like the Bible?** Over the years, some people have tried to stop the message of Jesus by making Bibles illegal. They have thought the Bible was an ordinary book about religion. Some rulers have torn the Bible to bits or even burned it. In some countries it is illegal to own a Bible. The U.S. does not allow teachers to teach the Bible in public schools. Sometimes it seems as though the Bible may go extinct. **Will it? Can it be destroyed?** No! It can never be destroyed because it is God's Word. It is not a trick. It is true. It will last forever.

Application: Invite a student to read Matthew 24:35 and Isaiah 40:8. **What difference does it make in a kid's life that God's Word will never pass away?** Kids can trust the truths of the Bible all their lives. Other things may change and become outdated, but not God's Word. **How does this help us trust God?**

Something Extra: Encourage the kids not to let their Bibles "become extinct" in their own lives. Challenge them to read the Bible every day for a whole week. Read two verses from Psalms each day. Think about it. Obey it.

Ideas for Use Anywhere

❑ Avoid this illustration if a trick candle is not available.

BIBLE STORY IDEAS

JOSIAH & THE BOOK OF THE LAW (2 Chronicles 34)
Even when God's Word was lost for a time, God caused the priests to find it. The people began obeying when they heard it again.

JEHOIAKIM BURNS THE SCROLL (Jeremiah 36)
Jehoiakim burned God's scroll. God gave his words to Jeremiah again.

Can't I learn about God from other books?

The Answer

The Bible is the only book in existence that tells us the exact truth about God because God, through the Holy Spirit, authored it.

Bible Proof

●●●**COLOSSIANS 2:8** See to it that no one takes you captive through hollow and deceptive philosophy, which depends on human tradition and the basic principles of this world rather than on Christ.

●●●**2 TIMOTHY 3:15b-16 -** You have known the holy Scriptures, which are able to make you wise for salvation through faith in Christ Jesus. All Scripture is God-breathed and is useful for teaching, rebuking, correcting, and training in righteousness.

Lesson Aim

To show that just as dirty water obscures the word "JESUS," other books hide the perfect, clear truth about Jesus, God's Son.

Before you teach ...

Kids today are taught to embrace every view of God as equally valid. There are no absolutes. Because of this, many believe the Bible is on the same level as every other spiritual book. But the Bible alone teaches the pure truth about God and his Son, Jesus!

Materials

❑ transparent container (glass or plastic) with water

❑ an index card reading "JESUS" in large letters

❑ clear plastic bag

❑ food coloring, juice, sauce, or dirt

❑ a mixing spoon

TO DO LIST:

❑ Gather materials.

❑ Write "JESUS" on the card. Tightly seal inside the plastic bag.

❑ Pray for your students!

? THE LESSON

Introduction: Discuss these questions. **What do your students like to learn from books? How many books can teach us the truth about God? Are these all equally true? What does each book say about Jesus? Is it different?** Give some examples of what different religious books teach about Jesus (The Koran – prophet, good man; The Book of Mormon – one of many gods, like us; etc.).

Demonstration: Show kids the container of water. Read the word "JESUS" on the card (in plastic inside the container). **Can they see it clearly?** Explain that this clarity is like reading the Bible. The Bible gives us a true picture of what Jesus is like, because the Bible is God's Word. Next, mix food coloring or juice into the water. Tell the kids to imagine that they are now reading a book that believes Jesus is a prophet but not God. **Is this what the Bible says?** The truth about Jesus cannot be seen clearly. Add more coloring and stir. Imagine we are reading a book that says Jesus was a good man and some of the things he said were interesting. **Is this what the Bible says?** No! Add the dirt and mix it in. Imagine we are reading a book that teaches that people or animals can be gods. It does not even mention Jesus. Explain that the truth about Jesus, which the Bible teaches so clearly, cannot even be seen now. These books totally cover up the truth about God.

Discussion: **When could you see the word "JESUS" the clearest? Why? Does any book, other than the Bible, teach the whole truth about Jesus? How can we tell if a book about God is truthful or not?** Compare it to the Bible.

Application: Read 2 Timothy 3:15b-16. **What does this verse tell us about who wrote the Bible?** It was God-breathed. **Why was it written?** The Bible's goal is to bring us to the knowledge of salvation, through faith in Christ Jesus, and to help us grow to be more like Jesus in everything we do.

Something Extra: Ask the kids to think of something they have been told about Jesus or God that they are not sure about. Challenge them to have a Christian adult help them find out what the Bible teaches about that subject.

Ideas for Use Anywhere

❑ Plastic zipper bags are not available in all areas. Use a regular plastic bag, or a small, clear jar to protect the card with the word "Jesus" on it.

BIBLE STORY IDEAS

SIMON THE SORCERER (Acts 8:9-25)
Simon mixed up truth from many religions to impress people. He learned the real truth about Jesus from Peter.

THE ETHIOPIAN (Acts 8:26-40)
The eunuch read God's Word. He did not understand. When Philip explained it, he wanted Jesus as his Savior. No other book's words can lead people to the truth about salvation.

PART 4

Questions about God and Sin

Why does God care if I sin?

Materials

☐ a roll of duct tape (or other tape or string)

The Answer

Sin makes a mess of our lives and traps us. God only wants the best for our lives, so he cares about keeping us from sinning.

Bible Proof

●●● **PROVERBS 5:22 -** The evil deeds of a wicked man ensnare him; the cords of his sin hold him fast.

●●● **HEBREWS 12:1b -** Let us throw off everything that hinders and the sin that so easily entangles, and let us run with perseverance the race marked out for us.

Lesson Aim

To show that just as a wad of duct tape is a mess that is impossible to untangle, sin makes a mess out of our lives. It is impossible for us to fix the mess ourselves.

Before you teach ...

God wants the very best for us. He knows that sin and disobedience tangle our lives. Even a little sin can have devastating effects. Today's lesson will give students a tangible demonstration of the consequences sin can have in their lives.

TO DO LIST:

☐ Roll up several long strips of duct tape into wadded balls.

 THE LESSON

Introduction: **How many of you have ever thought, said or done something that wasn't very nice?** *(Raise your hand, as well.)* **What is the name for doing wrong things like this?** Sin. Some sins do not seem like a problem. They seem harmless. We wonder why God cares. **Why do you think God cares if we sin?**

Demonstration: Invite several students to participate in an experiment. Give each a wad of duct tape. Instruct each to try to be the first to unroll the ball. Watch them work furiously for several minutes. Enjoy their antics. Some may partially unravel a ball. Point out that the tape is still messy and unusable.

Discussion: **Does sin really affect us?** These wads of tape remind us of the effects of sin. **How does sin affect us?** Sin messes up our hearts and lives. It tangles us on the inside and causes problem in our lives that are difficult to get out of. Sin can keep us from being useful to God or anyone else. **Remember the duct tape? What happens when we try to fix our sin?** The worst news about sin is that it is impossible for us to fix on our own. We need help. The best news is that Jesus came to rescue us. He will forgive our sin, but we must do something first. We must ask. We must have a sorry attitude. We must want to be forgiven. We must admit we were wrong. We must confess our sin.

Application: Invite students to privately consider answers to the following questions. **Is there anything you do that you know is wrong but keep doing anyway? How does it affect others around you?** *(Show the wad of tape.)* **Does your life feel like this on the inside?** Jesus wants to help. **Are you ready to ask him for his help?** Read 1 John 1:9. Let students privately pray to ask God for forgiveness.

Something Extra: Each day, at the end of the day, for one week straight, challenge students to ask God to forgive them for any sins they have committed. **How do your students feel at the end of the week? Do they feel clean now?** Confessing our sin gives us freedom and joy on the inside.

Ideas for Use Anywhere

❑ Duct tape is not available in many places around the world. Use another type of tape, or string.

❑ Use only two students, instead of many.

BIBLE STORY IDEAS

SAUL REJECTED AS KING (1 Samuel 15)
Saul disobeyed Samuel, God's messenger and judge. His heart was rebellious and selfish. His sin led him to be a miserable man.

JONAH (Jonah 1-4)
Jonah ran from God. He did not want to obey. He sinned. God cared. Jonah's disobedience was keeping the people of Nineveh from loving God.

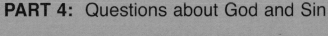

Why is a little sin such a big deal to God?

Materials

❑ a facial tissue

The Answer

God knows that even a little sin is bad for us. It hurts our lives now and for eternity when we sin.

Bible Proof

●●● **ROMANS 6:23 -** For the wages of sin is death, but the gift of God is eternal life in Christ Jesus our Lord.

●●● **JAMES 2:10 -** For whoever keeps the whole law and yet stumbles at just one point is guilty of breaking all of it.

Lesson Aim

To show that just as a few germs can make a tissue unclean, a little bit of sin makes our hearts unclean.

Before you teach ...

Teachers avoid talking about sin. It's so ... politically incorrect. But not in God's kingdom. In fact, a full understanding of God's love, forgiveness, and grace are impossible without an understanding of the gravity of sin in God's eyes. Let your kids know you do not enjoy talking about sin, but remind them that it is important to God, so you need to talk about it together. Lead them to discover what great love God showed when he sent Jesus to pay for our sin.

TO DO LIST:

❑ Pray for your students.

❑ Think of a personal story to share about how a little sin hurt a lot of people.

? THE LESSON

Introduction: Show students the tissue. **What can you tell me about this tissue?** It is nice and clean. It could be used to clean off a dish, wipe a tear, or clean a small cut.

Demonstration: Blow your nose, ever so slightly, into the tissue. Next, offer it to one of your students. Show that there is hardly anything on it. It is almost new. Look at all the clean spaces. Show the dry spots. Try to convince one or two students to take the tissue. **Why doesn't anyone want it?** Because it has germs. Just a few germs make the whole thing dirty and unclean.

Discussion: Some kids may wonder, **why is a little sin such a big deal to God?** If kids do not murder or tell big lies or hurt people, they may feel that they are pretty good. However, according to God, a little bit of sin makes us unclean and unholy to God. He knows it is not good for us. He wants us to be clean of sin, to be forgiven through Christ. This is also the only way we can come close to God.

Application: Invite a student to read Romans 6:23. **What is God's penalty for sin (even a little)?** Death. **Is there any way to fix the problem?** Yes, by asking Jesus Christ to forgive our sin and believing he does it. **Do you have something to talk with God about?** He will forgive any sin, if we ask him to (1 John 1:9).

Something Extra: Divide students into small groups. Challenge each group to come up with a list of "little sins" kids think are okay, but that God considers wrong. Include stealing cookies, taking money from mother's purse, disobeying parents, not cleaning a room when supposed to, telling little lies, etc. Realize that spilling milk, getting a low grade on a test, etc. are NOT necessarily sin. **Who comes up with the longest list?**

Ideas for Use Anywhere

❑ In some cultures, concepts about germs may not be the same as for North Americans, making this lesson unusable. Or, children might take the tissue, in order not to be wasteful. Check it out.

BIBLE STORY IDEAS

ZACCHAEUS (Luke 19:1-19)
God forgave him for his sin of cheating people for their money.

GEHAZI IS GREEDY (2 Kings 5)
Elisha's servant lied to get a few clothes and a little money. He became leprous for the rest of his life because of his sin.

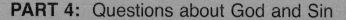

Aren't some sins worse than others?

Materials

☐ index cards or papers with a different sin listed on each *(see suggested list on page 51)*

The Answer

No. All sin is despicable in God's eyes. If we have committed one sin, we have broken all of God's law.

Bible Proof

●●●**JAMES 2:10 -** For whoever keeps the whole law and yet stumbles at just one point is guilty of breaking all of it.

●●●**ISAIAH 64:6 -** All of us have become like one who is unclean, and all our righteous acts are like filthy rags; we all shrivel up like a leaf, and like the wind our sins sweep us away.

Lesson Aim

To show that although people may think of some sins as worse than others, God sees all sin the same … as breaking his law.

Before you teach …

People tend to rank sin. We justify our wrongs, thinking they must not be a big deal to God. But they are. All sins are despicable in God's eyes and deserving of death! Breaking one of God's laws, even in a small way, is equal to breaking every law. Kids need to know that God takes sin very seriously; so seriously, in fact, that he sent his own Son to pay the price for all our sins, "little" and "big," to be forgiven forever.

TO DO LIST:

☐ Gather materials needed.

☐ Write one sin on each card or paper.

☐ Pray for your students to understand!

 **THE LESSON**

Introduction: Tell your students that sin is a big deal to God. Even though it may not be pleasant to talk about, we need to discuss it because it separates us from God. Today's lesson will help your kids learn an important truth about sin. Start by asking the question: **Which sins are the worst?**

Demonstration: Show the cards. Read them out loud. Ask each student to select a card from the pile and hold it up against their chest for others to see. Invite students, without your help, to arrange themselves in order of worst to "not so bad" sins.

> ## List of Sins
> *(write one per card or paper)*
> Murder
> Stealing a piece of gum
> Lying in a court of law
> Lying to your teacher
> Cheating on a test
> Calling someone a bad name
> Sticking your tongue out at a
>   sister or brother
> Disobeying your parent
> Littering *(may not be
>   considered a sin)*

Discussion: **Why did you put the sins in this order?** Some sins seem to hurt more people than others. Other sins seem harmless. **What order would God put them in?** Invite a student to read James 2:10. **What does the Bible say about sin?** If we have sinned just once, we have broken the whole entire law. Wow! It also tells us that all sin deserves the same punishment: death. **So, are some sins worse than others?** No, they are equally bad. The good news is Jesus did not die to just take away some of the sins or to take away only the ones that do not hurt as many people. He came to take away all the sins of the world! (Gather all cards.) Read Romans 6:23 together.

Application: **Which sins have you done that you did not really think were all that bad? Can you think of some ways they actually do hurt other people? Do you want to tell God you are sorry for what you have done?** Invite students to spend time in quiet, personal prayer, asking God to forgive big, little and in-between sins.

> ## Ideas for Use Anywhere
>
> ❑ In some areas around the world, attention to sin is severe. Kids in North America tend to need this lesson more than international friends.
>
> ❑ Cartoons may not be available for some kids.

Something Extra: Watch a cartoon on TV or DVD. Look for "sins" that characters commit. **Do people who do not know God think these are sin? Which do they think are "no big deal"?**

BIBLE STORY IDEA
ADAM AND EVE EAT A LITTLE FRUIT (Genesis 3) Eating the fruit of a tree may not seem like a big deal. But sin is sin. There were huge consequences for their behavior.

Why do bad people get away with doing wrong?

Materials

- ❑ a large block of ice on a tray
- ❑ towels
- ❑ rock salt or table salt

The Answer

They don't. For a while, it may seem as if no one sees them or catches them, but sin always harms their hearts and their relationship with God. All will eventually be judged by God.

Bible Proof

●●● **2 PETER 2:13 -** They will be paid back with harm for the harm they have done ...

●●● **JAMES 1:15 -** Then, after desire has conceived, it gives birth to sin; and sin, when it is full-grown, gives birth to death.

Lesson Aim

To show that just like salt, over time, ruins a block of ice, sin, over time (even when no one else knows about it), ruins our hearts.

Before you teach ...

Kids who do bad things and do not have to pay any consequences for their actions are often the kids who are admired and thought of as cool. It seems like they get away with everything and even profit from their sinfulness. Though people seem to get away with sinful behavior without consequences, they don't. Sin rots a person from the inside out. Sin starts by spoiling a person's heart, and it eventually will ruin the rest of their life. God's Word also tells us that, in the end, he will judge all people for what they have done.

TO DO LIST:

- ❑ If you are short on time in class, place a handful of salt on the ice block about 20 minutes before the lesson so it melts a hole in the ice. Cover with a towel until ready for demonstration.

- ❑ Gather other materials.

52

 # THE LESSON

Introduction: **Do you know any kids who do bad things?** Do not name them aloud! **Do they get away with doing wrong? Why does God let them "get away with sin"?** Today's demonstration will help us understand what really happens to bad people who seem to get away with doing wrong.

Demonstration: Show the non-salted block of ice. Tell students to imagine it is a kid who sins a lot and seems to get away with it. Have them pretend the salt represents sin. Invite a few students to name a sin the imaginary kid might have committed. Let students sprinkle salt on the ice as they name a sin. When each student has had a chance to add salt to the ice, tell your students this kid has not asked Jesus to take away his sin. He has not been caught. Set the block aside to check on later. After at least fifteen minutes, look at the block again. **What changes have occurred to the ice? What is happening to the inside of the ice?** A big ugly hole has formed. The salt has ruined the inside of the block.

Discussion: **Is this anything like our hearts when we sin? How?** When we sin our pure hearts are spoiled on the inside. Sin destroys the love and happiness in our hearts. Sin destroys us from the inside out. Sin breaks our relationship with God. Invite your students to read 2 Peter 2:13 and James 1:15. **Do people who do bad things really get away with it?** No!

Application: **Have you ever done something wrong that no one else knew about? How did you feel?** Every sin will have a consequence; God will see to it. God is also hoping people will repent. **Do you need to ask God to forgive you for doing wrong?**

Something Extra: Invite each student to think of a person who does bad things and gets away with it. It may be a neighborhood bully or someone they have learned about in the news. Pray for that person every day for a week. Ask God to help them see their sin and repent. Ask God to also help them learn about forgiveness through Jesus and receive him as their Savior.

Ideas for Use Anywhere

☐ In a variety of teaching settings, including rural areas around the world, ice will not be readily available for this lesson.

BIBLE STORY IDEAS

AHAB AND NABOTH'S VINEYARD (1 Kings 16:29-34; 19:1; 21:1) Ahab selfishly, but quietly, had Naboth murdered so he could take his vineyard. God saw. In the end, Ahab died a terrible death.

HAMAN (Esther 3, 5, 7)
Haman plotted to destroy the Jews. It seemed he was getting away with his plan. God saw him and rewarded him for his behavior.

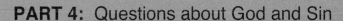

If I really try hard, can't I be good all the time?

Materials

- ☐ anyone with two good legs
- ☐ erasable board or paper and writing supplies (optional)

The Answer

No! It is impossible for a person not to sin. Therefore, no one can be perfect all the time.

Bible Proof

- ●●●**ROMANS 3:10b-12 -** There is no one righteous, not even one; there is no one who understands, no one who seeks God. All have turned away, they have together become worthless; there is no one who does good, not even one.
- ●●●**ROMANS 3:23 -** For all have sinned and fall short of the glory of God.
- ●●●**TITUS 3:5a -** He saved us, not because of righteous things we had done, but because of his mercy.

Lesson Aim

To show that just as it is impossible to stand on one foot forever, it is impossible for people not to sin and so to earn their own way to heaven.

Before you teach ...

Kids know they want to be good. They try. In fact, most kids think they are good almost all the time. For some, they may even begin to think that if only they try hard enough, they can really be perfect all the time. Good, maybe. Sinless, no. This, in fact, is the reason God sent his Son, Jesus. No matter how hard we try, we cannot be perfect. We cannot earn salvation. Only Jesus was perfect. And he paid the price for our forgiveness forever.

TO DO LIST:

- ☐ No special preparations this time.
- ☐ Pray for your students by name.

 THE LESSON

Introduction: Notice aloud that your students look like very good kids. In fact, they look great! **What good things have you done this week?** List some on an erasable board or paper, if you wish. Celebrate them. **Can any of us be good all the time? Can we be perfect?** Try an experiment to find the answer.

Demonstration: Invite the entire class to stand and join a contest. See who can stand on one leg for the longest time. One foot stands on the floor. The second foot may never touch anything else: the ground, the other foot, the wall, or a friend. Students might want to sing a song while waiting. **Can anyone stand like this forever?** (This may take a while to be determined!)

Discussion: **Is it possible for any person to keep their second foot off the ground forever? Why not?** People need two legs to balance. They are not strong enough to stand on one leg forever. Look in the Bible to see what else is impossible for people to do. Have students look up Romans 3:10 and Romans 3:23. The Bible tells us it is impossible for people not to sin. We all break God's laws. Only one person had the power and strength not to sin, ever. Jesus, God's only Son, was perfect! He was also able to pay the price for all our sin to be forgiven when he died on the cross for us.

Application: **Have you accepted God's gift of forgiveness through Jesus? Would you like to today?** Pray with students who would like to receive Jesus as their Savior. **If we can't be perfect, why try to be good?** Our goodness cannot earn our way to heaven. But becoming more like Christ is God's plan for us. As we love him, we want to be more like Jesus. God helps us to grow as we obey.

Something Extra: Invite each student to write out one of the following verses. Think about it. Try to obey it for a week. **Was it easy?**

❑Matthew 5:48   ❑Matthew 5:44
❑Matthew 7:12   ❑Matthew 6:25

Ideas for Use Anywhere

❑Watch out for kids in great shape who could stand all day. Set a time limit, in case some could do this for hours!

❑In some areas, writing supplies may be scarce. Discuss answers orally.

BIBLE STORY IDEAS

SAUL'S CONVERSION (Acts 9:1-19)
Saul tried very hard to follow all God's laws. He finally realized his need to believe in Jesus Christ as his Savior.

MOSES DISOBEYS GOD (Numbers 20:1-12, 27:12-14)
Moses was a remarkable leader. He received the Ten Commandments. Nevertheless, he disobeyed God, as all people will.

How do I know God forgives me?

Materials

- ❑ a clear pitcher of water
- ❑ package of Kool-Aid®, unsweetened
- ❑ laundry bleach
- ❑ a picture of a cross
- ❑ a stirring spoon

The Answer

The Bible tells us so. God totally forgives us through Jesus when we ask him to.

Bible Proof

●●● **PSALM 103:12 -** As far as the east is from the west, so far has he removed our transgressions from us.

●●● **1 JOHN 1:9 -** If we confess our sins, he is faithful and just and will forgive us our sins and purify us from all unrighteousness.

Lesson Aim

To show that just as bleach can make colored water clear again, God's forgiveness clears our hearts of sin.

Before you teach ...

Kids are taught to forgive, but they usually do not forgive and forget. They, like the rest of us, store up the memory of past hurts in their hearts. Does not God remember all the things we have done wrong, too? After all, he is smarter than the rest of us. Actually, the Bible teaches us that God's forgiveness is not like human forgiveness. It is perfect.

TO DO LIST:

- ❑ Fill the pitcher with water.
- ❑ Gather materials.
- ❑ Tell of a time you were thankful for God's forgiveness.

THE LESSON

Introduction: **Have you ever been hurt by a friend? How did you feel? Have you forgiven him or her? Do you still remember what they did?** It is hard for us to forgive and forget when people hurt our feelings. **What about God? Does he forget our sin?** He is so smart, he must remember it all. This demonstration will help us understand the answer.

Demonstration: Show students the container of water. Enjoy looking through the clear water. Add the Kool-Aid®. **What happened to our nice clear water?** The water is murky. **Is there any way to clean our water again with our fingers?** No, it would be impossible to clean the juice out on our own. We need help. We need ... a Kool-Aid® cleaning professional. Show the bleach. Ask the students' permission to clean the Kool-Aid® out of the water. Pour in some bleach and stir well. Watch the water clear up. The color is all gone.

Discussion: Tell the students the water is like our hearts. It is supposed to be clean and clear and ready to be used for important things, such as loving others. The Kool-Aid® is like sin. **What happens when sin enters our hearts?** Sin does more than just color our hearts, it pollutes it. **Is it possible for us to get the sin out of our hearts by ourselves?** No, it is impossible. We need the sin cleaning professional: JESUS! (Show a cross, if available.) Jesus died on the cross for our sins. When we confess our sin and ask him for forgiveness, he forgives us and forgets it forever. *(NOTE: Plan for safe disposal of liquid after the demonstration.)*

Application: **Have you accepted God's forgiveness through Jesus?** Jesus paid a big price to cleanse you from sin! **Will you let him do it?**

Something Extra: While enjoying a glass of real Kool-Aid®, invite students to each write a private list naming things they have done wrong. Ask God for forgiveness. Then tear up and throw away the lists. God has cleaned it away. It is remembered no more.

Ideas for Use Anywhere

❑ Kool-Aid® may not be available. Use other juice or concentrate that responds to bleach.

❑ For "Something Extra", activity may be done mentally, without paper.

BIBLE STORY IDEAS

JESUS HEALS A PARALYTIC (Mark 2:1-12)
Jesus not only healed a crippled man so he could walk, but he also forgave the man's sins.

THE CRUCIFIXION (Matthew 27:32-56)
Jesus died on the cross so the price to forgive our sin could be paid forever. If we confess our sin, he will forgive us.

What does God think of me when I sin?

Materials

❑ cool sunglasses (as many as possible)

The Answer

God detests sin, but loves sinners. He looks at us through the work Jesus did on the cross.

Bible Proof

●●● **ROMANS 5:8 -** But God demonstrates his own love for us in this: While we were still sinners, Christ died for us.

●●● **2 CORINTHIANS 5:21 -** God made him who had no sin to be sin for us, so that in him we might become the righteousness of God.

Lesson Aim

To show that just as sunglasses filter out some of the sun's rays, God looks at our lives through the filter of Jesus' work on the cross.

Before you teach ...

It's amazing. Our sin is detestable to God and, because we all sin, we should be unable to enjoy a relationship with God forever. But God had different plans. His love compelled him to send Jesus to die on the cross for us. Those who receive the forgiveness he purchased there are seen by God in a whole new way. They are seen as totally clean and pure, without sin. What happened? The filter of Jesus' blood and sacrifice changes God's view forever. It's amazing!

TO DO LIST:

❑ Gather sunglasses or prepare simple "sunglass" rectangles with colored cellophane.

❑ Pray for your students!

 THE LESSON

Introduction: Ask your students what God thinks of sin. He hates it. He can't be around it. He detests it. **Why?** Because he is a holy God. **Then what does God think of us when we sin?**

Demonstration: Invite a volunteer to try on a pair of sunglasses. Ask the student to describe to the class how things looked before and after they put the glasses on. Let as many kids as possible have a turn. **Do things look exactly as they really are when wearing the glasses?** We can see the same objects, but the color is different.

Discussion: **How is this like the way in which God sees us?** Even though God hates sin, God looks at those who have received Jesus as their Savior through the filter of Jesus' blood. What this means is that the sacrifice Jesus made on the cross paid the price for our sin to be forgiven. **Does God not see the truth?** Yes. He sees the truth. But when we have been forgiven, the truth is that our hearts are pure and clean through Christ. God sees no sin.

Application: **Have you ever felt badly for doing something wrong? Have you thought God did not love you anymore?** The truth is that God always loves us. He never stops loving us, even when we sin. **Why is this such good news? Will God always love you?** Yes!

Something Extra: Every time your students notice someone wearing sunglasses in the coming week, invite them to think about God. **Does God love them at that moment? How does God see them? Do they need to ask forgiveness for a wrong?**

Ideas for Use Anywhere

❑Children may take turns looking through one pair of sunglasses.

❑If sunglasses are not available, invite children to look through a thin cloth or veil.

BIBLE STORY IDEAS

THE CALLING OF MATTHEW (Matthew 9:9-13) Matthew had been a tax collector. It was an impure occupation. Jesus saw him and invited him to become his follower. Eventually, Matthew wrote a book of the Bible.

PARABLE OF THE PHARISEE AND TAX COLLECTOR (Luke 18:9-14) God looks at people's hearts to see whether they trust in him to forgive their sin or not. Those who trust in Jesus are seen as totally clean before God, no matter what they have done before.

PART 5

Questions about God and Jesus

How is Jesus different from other people?

Materials

- ❑ non-inflated balloons (or feathers)
- ❑ a friend

The Answer

Hundreds of predictions about the Messiah, made hundreds of years before Christ was born, all came true in Jesus!

Bible Proof

- ●●● **HEBREWS 1:1-2 -** In the past God spoke to our forefathers through the prophets at many times and in various ways, but in these last days he has spoken to us by his Son, whom he appointed heir of all things, and through whom he made the universe.
- ●●● **ACTS 2:23-24a -** This man was handed over to you by God's set purpose and foreknowledge; and you, with the help of wicked men, put him to death by nailing him to a cross. But God raised him from the dead.

Lesson Aim

To show that just as it is impossible to predict where a balloon will land with 100% accuracy, it would be impossible for hundreds of predictions about a Messiah to all be true in one man, unless God caused it to happen, as he did in Jesus.

Before you teach ...

Today, your students will have a chance to learn one incredible fact that makes Jesus different from all others. There were hundreds of predictions about the Messiah. They all came true in Jesus. No one who made these predictions could have caused them to come true with their own abilities. God sent Jesus to be the promised Messiah. This is one huge difference between Jesus and the rest of the human race.

TO DO LIST:

- ❑ Pray for your children by name.

 THE LESSON

Introduction: **Who is Jesus? What do people think about him? How is Jesus different from ordinary people?** These balloons will help us understand how Old Testament prophecies teach us that Jesus is extraordinary.

Demonstration: Have students each choose a partner. They take turns with this demonstration. The first students place their partners on one side of the room. Next, the first students return to the opposite side of the room, and each inflate a balloon. Let go of the untied balloons. Students try to see if their balloons will land on their partners. **Did all the balloons go where you wanted them to go?** Trade places and try again. **Did anyone hit their target accurately? Why? Why not?**

Discussion: Predictions about the future are hard to make. Hundreds of predictions in the Old Testament told about a coming Messiah/King. Read several prophecies from the Old Testament. **Would it be possible for you to make any of these predictions come true? Did your** balloon do what you wanted? Over 300 predictions, written at least 400 years before his birth, all came true in Jesus. Read several New Testament fulfillments. **Could they have all come true by accident? Could the writers of the predictions have made them come true?** No! It would be impossible. But God could. This is a big part of what makes Jesus different. His exact birth and ministry had been planned hundreds of years before he was born.

Prophecies about Jesus

Old Testament Prophecy	New Testament Fulfillment
Micah 5:2	Luke 2:4 & 6
Isaiah 7:14	Matthew 1:23-25
Zechariah 9:9	Matthew 21:4-8
Psalm 22:6-8	Mark 15:29-32
Psalm 22:18	Mark 15:24

Application: God went out of his way to send Jesus to save us. **Do you believe it? Have you responded to receive him as your Savior and King?**

Ideas for Use Anywhere

❑ In many areas, balloons are not available. Use feathers or a small piece of lightweight cloth.

BIBLE STORY IDEAS

SIMEON SEES JESUS IN THE TEMPLE (Luke 2:21-35)
God promised Simeon would see the Messiah before he died. Simeon knew he had seen this promised person when he saw Jesus.

THE TRIUMPHAL ENTRY (Matthew 21:1-11)
Jesus entered Jerusalem, fulfilling prophecy as he went. He is the Messiah!

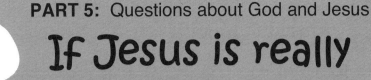

If Jesus is really alive, why can't I see him?

Materials

☐ one large blanket

The Answer

Jesus is alive in heaven, preparing a place for us. We can still see him at work by how he affects people's lives.

Bible Proof

●●●**JOHN 14:2-3 -** In my Father's house are many rooms; if it were not so, I would have told you. I am going there to prepare a place for you. And if I go and prepare a place for you, I will come back and take you to be with me ...

●●●**JOHN 14:19a & 20b -** Before long, the world will not see me anymore, but you will see me ... I am in my Father, and you are in me, and I am in you.

Lesson Aim

To show that even when a person is hidden from us he can still be alive. Even though we cannot see Jesus physically, now, we can know he is alive by how he affects people's lives through the Holy Spirit.

Before you teach ...

Kids have difficulty knowing what is real and what is not. Kids are very concrete thinkers. Kids wonder, is Jesus pretend, like Santa Claus. Will they stop believing in him when they grow up? How can they know he is real? It is especially difficult since they do not see Jesus in the news or in person. One way kids can know Jesus is real is by watching the way he affects people's lives, including their own.

TO DO LIST:

☐ Pray for your students.

☐ Tell of a time you recognized Christ's presence in your own life.

? THE LESSON

Introduction: Ask your students how many of them have ever seen Jesus. **Where? If Jesus is really alive, why can't we see him? How can we know he is real and is alive?** Today's lesson will help us consider this.

Demonstration: Ask for a volunteer who does not mind the dark. Cover this volunteer with the blanket. **Can we see him?** No! **Is he alive? How do we know?** Ask the volunteer to crawl around, still wearing the blanket. He or she may brush up against the other students and move something on a table. **Now can we see him? How do we know he's alive?** We can see how he or she affects things. **What happens if we have our eyes shut or we turn away from him?** It is much harder to see, but we can still hear or feel movements. Thank your volunteer and remove the blanket.

Discussion: How is this like Jesus? Ask a student to read John 14:19a and 20b. **How can we "see" Jesus even if we can't see him with our eyes?** We can see how he affects people's lives. **What kind of difference does Jesus make in people's lives? How are you different because Jesus is in you and with you?**

Application: Do you have Jesus in you and with you? Every person can ask him to be, today. **Are you letting Jesus affect your life? Are you asking him to help and guide you? Are you praying to him? Are you looking for his answers?** We can miss seeing him and how he is working if we are not looking or if we are not willing to obey his quiet voice as he speaks to our hearts.

Ideas for Use Anywhere

- ❑ Crawling on the floor may be culturally unacceptable in some areas. Check first.

- ❑ If Santa Claus is not known, substitute another fictional, local childhood character.

- ❑ Change the "Something Extra" activity to a class activity with shared response.

Something Extra: Invite students to start a prayer journal this week. Write down specific prayers each day and be watching to see how Jesus affects the lives of the people and the situations your students pray for.

BIBLE STORY IDEAS

CENTURION'S SERVANT HEALED (Matthew 8:5-13)
Jesus did not have to be physically present to heal the centurion's servant. He simply spoke the words. He can help us, too.

JESUS' ASCENSION (Acts 1:1-11)
Jesus went to be with God in heaven. His power extends to us, even though he is not physically present in a body. He sent his Holy Spirit to be in us and with us always.

PART 5: Questions about God and Jesus

Why did Jesus come to earth, anyway?

Materials

❑ a gem or jewel (real or fake)

The Answer

He loves us! We are like priceless gems to God. God paid a big price when he sent Jesus to die for us.

Bible Proof

●●● **1 JOHN 4:10 -** This is love: not that we loved God, but that he loved us and sent his Son as an atoning sacrifice for our sins.

●●● **JOHN 3:16 -** For God so loved the world that he gave his one and only Son that whoever believes in him shall not perish but have eternal life.

Lesson Aim

To show that just as a gem is of such great value that, if it is lost, we will do almost anything to get it back, each person is so valuable to Jesus that he was willing to come to earth and pay the price for us to be reconciled to God.

Before you teach ...

Some kids who go to church (and kids who don't) do not realize the reason Jesus came to earth. Some may think he was just another interesting holy man. Many may not realize the great sacrifice Jesus endured, leaving his position in heaven as Lord over all, to become a common man and die for us. Why did he do it? Because we are so valuable to him! We are his greatest treasure, and saving us was his whole reason for coming.

TO DO LIST:

❑ Pray for your students by name.

 # THE LESSON

Introduction: Begin the lesson by asking students why they think Jesus came to earth. **If he is God and rules everything from heaven, why would he want to come to earth? Did he come because he was curious about people?** Today's demonstration will help us understand a huge reason for his coming.

Demonstration: Show your gem to the students. Pass it around and let each kid hold it very carefully. If it is fake, tell them to imagine it is real. **How would you care for this gem? Would you keep it in a safe place? Would you sell it?** Some people say gems are priceless. **What does priceless mean?** Priceless means "so valuable that no amount of money would be enough to buy it." **What would you do if a priceless gem was stolen or lost?** Most people would search for it until they found it. They might even spend lots of money hiring detectives to help them get it back. **How would you feel if you lost it and then got it back?** Overjoyed!

Discussion: Every person is like a priceless gem to God. He loves us and wants us to be safe and near him. Because of sin, we are separated from God. It is as if we were lost. **What did God do to save us for himself?** God paid a big price when he sent Jesus to die for us. He made a way for our sins to be forgiven, so we could be close to God. He is overjoyed when we receive Jesus as our Lord and Savior. He loves us so much. This is why Jesus came.

Application: Have you received Jesus as your Lord and Savior? He paid a big price for your sins. **Would you like to come close to God today?** Some kids have already received Jesus' forgiveness. **Have you thanked him lately for what he has done for you? Are you staying close to Jesus, who paid such a big price for you? Are you spending time with him, praying and learning more about him?** Every person is so priceless; Jesus wants to be close to us always.

Something Extra: In the coming week, challenge students to thank Jesus for what he did. One way to thank him is by telling other people what he did for them. **Can you tell someone else that Jesus thinks they are as valuable as a gem?**

Ideas for Use Anywhere

❑ Check into gems or jewels that might be available in your local community. Avoid using family heirlooms or other non-replaceable treasures.

BIBLE STORY IDEAS

PARABLE OF THE LOST SHEEP (Luke 15:1-7)
Jesus loves kids so much. He does not want even one to be lost.

PARABLES OF TREASURE (Matthew 13:44-46)
Jesus paid a big price to purchase us, the people he created, as his priceless treasure.

Was Jesus really from God?

Materials

❏ one fancy robe or coat (fur, rhinestones, etc.)

❏ one old ordinary bathrobe or shirt

The Answer

Yes! God sent Jesus to be king of all kings, showing his great love for his people by first becoming their humble servant.

Bible Proof

●●●**PHILIPPIANS 2:5b-8 -** Christ Jesus: Who, being in very nature God, … made himself nothing, taking the very nature of a servant … humbled himself and became obedient to death – even death on a cross!

●●●**JOHN 17:3 -** Now this is eternal life: that they may know you, the only true God, and Jesus Christ whom you have sent.

Lesson Aim

To show that just as robes can be changed, Jesus set aside his glory to become an ordinary human being like us.

Before you teach ...

Important people dress just the right way. They make sure they are seen with the right people. They are powerful and influential. But your kids need to know that looks can be deceiving. Jesus was more important than any ruler or movie star, but he did not dress the part. Though he created the universe, he came to earth as a humble child, lived in poverty and died the death of a criminal. He loved us a lot to do this.

TO DO LIST:

❏ There are no special preparations.

❏ Pray for your students.

68

?THE LESSON

Introduction: Ask students to name some of the people they admire the most. **Who would you like to meet?** Think about sports heroes, musicians, movie stars, rulers of countries or wealthy people. **What is it about these people that makes them so great? What kind of houses do they live in? What kind of cars do they drive? Do they wear ordinary clothes or fancy clothes? What about Jesus? Where was he born? What did he use for transportation? What kind of clothes did he wear? Was he really important?**

Demonstration: Invite a volunteer to come up and put on the fancy robe or coat. **What kind of person would wear this coat?** Someone rich or important. Next, ask the same person to put on the old bathrobe or shirt. **What kind of person would wear this?** Someone ordinary, common, not rich. **What happened to the person wearing the robe? Did he or she change personalities?** NO! The volunteer just changed outfits. Inside, he or she is still the same person.

Discussion: **How is this like Jesus? Who was Jesus before he came to earth?** He was God over all, King of kings and Lord of lords. **What changed when he came to earth?** He did not come dressed in fancy clothes or looking important, but he was still God underneath his common, ordinary human body. **Why do you think he came looking like a normal person?** He did not want people to be afraid to get close to him. He wanted to come as a servant, to die on the cross to take away our sin. He came to show us how he wants us to live: humbly, as servants. God wanted people to be attracted to his love for us, not the clothes he wore.

Application: Invite a student to read Philippians 2:5-8. Even though Jesus seemed ordinary, he was a King, God's Son. He showed God's power and God's wisdom. Mostly, he showed God's love by giving it all up to come and save us. Thank him together.

Ideas for Use Anywhere

❑ Use clothing that kids in the local culture will associate with honor or riches and with ordinary simplicity. These may not be the same for kids in your community.

Something Extra: Challenge kids to give up something they love in the coming week. **Is it easy? How could Jesus give up heaven for us?** We must mean A LOT to him.

BIBLE STORY IDEA

THE REQUEST OF JAMES & JOHN (Mark 10:35-41) James and John wanted seats of honor. Jesus reminded them that following him is all about serving one another, just as Jesus served us.

Can I believe in God – and not Jesus?

Materials

❑ several keys

❑ one item that can be opened by one of the above keys

The Answer

No! The Bible teaches there is only one way to God, and that is by believing in Jesus as Lord and Savior.

Bible Proof

●●● **JOHN 14:6 -** Jesus answered, "I am the way and the truth and the life. No one comes to the Father except through me."

●●● **I JOHN 2:23 -** No one who denies the Son has the Father; whoever acknowledges the Son has the Father also.

Lesson Aim

To discuss that just as only one special key enables us to open a lock, only belief in Jesus can enable us to know the one true God.

Before you teach ...

In today's society, people like to think that all religions lead us to the same place. But it is not true. We are not brought close to God by a religion or by being good. We are not even brought close to God because we think God might exist. We can only be brought close to the true God by a person, Christ Jesus. Belief in him is the key to reaching God.

TO DO LIST:

❑ Nearby, hide the object that the key opens.

❑ Gather other materials.

❑ Pray for your students!

 **THE LESSON**

Introduction: How do different people think we get to heaven? Take some time and listen to several answers. Many kids may say they must be good enough. Others may say it is a simple belief in God's existence. Today's demonstration will help us learn what the Bible teaches about this.

Demonstration: Show students the keys. Let them touch and feel them all, if possible. Invite kids to guess what the keys might be used for. Now, get out the item that one of the keys will open, the one with a lock. **Will all of these keys fit this lock?** Have each student try the key they are holding. Choose the student holding the key that works to go last. Celebrate when the lock is opened.

Discussion: How is this key like Jesus? Some people believe that there are many ways to God and heaven, but the Bible teaches us something different. **Are Bible words different from other words?** Yes. They are God's true words. **Should we pay attention to the Bible?** Yes! Invite a student to read John 14:6 and 1 John 2:23. **According to the Bible, can you believe in God without believing in Jesus?** No. Jesus is the only one who can help us know the one true God. The Bible tells us that, without belief in Jesus, we do not really know God. Jesus is the one key that leads us to God. He is the only way.

Application: Jesus is even better than a key to a treasure chest. He is the key to a lifetime friendship with the God of the universe. What an awesome treasure! **Do you want that treasure? Do you have the key?**

Ideas for Use Anywhere

❑Keys and locks should be available worldwide. Substitute a box tied with a rope and knot, if no lock and key are available.

❑Check local religious backdrops before sending children to share Christ with friends. Prepare children with a loving attitude and clear information first.

Challenge: Ask students if they have friends who might believe in God but do not believe in Jesus. Challenge students to share one of this lesson's verses with a friend this coming week and tell them about the one key to a friendship with God, forever. **How does the friend respond?** Discuss friendship evangelism.

BIBLE STORY IDEAS

PETER AND CORNELIUS (Acts 10:22-48)
Peter learned that God has called people from all races and nations to know Christ. Jesus' name is the only name by which we can be saved.

PHILIP AND THE ETHIOPIAN (Acts 8:26-39)
The Ethiopian had just worshiped God at the temple in Jerusalem, but Philip told him he needed to receive Jesus. He did.

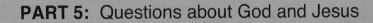

Is Jesus REALLY God?

Materials

❑ two outwardly identical balloons: one filled with helium, one filled with regular air

The Answer

Yes, Jesus really is God! We know because he showed God's power, especially when he rose from the dead.

Bible Proof

●●● **JOHN 20:27-28 -** Then he said to Thomas, "Put your finger here; see my hands. Reach out your hand and put it into my side. Stop doubting and believe." Thomas said to him, "My Lord and My God!"

●●● **MATTHEW 11:3-5 -** "Are you the one who was to come?" … Jesus replied, "Go back and report to John what you hear and see: The blind receive sight, the lame walk, those who have leprosy are cured, the deaf hear, the dead are raised, and the good news is preached to the poor."

●●● **JOHN 8:58b -** Jesus answered, "before Abraham was born, I am!"

Lesson Aim

To show that just as two balloons can look the same on the outside and be totally different inside, Jesus, who looked like an ordinary human, is God.

Before you teach ...

Jesus was a man in every way, but inside he was also extraordinary. How can they know he is real? He demonstrated all God's attributes, including his power, love and wisdom. The clincher came when he predicted his own death and resurrection, then fulfilled the prediction. No other religious leader can claim this divine power.

TO DO LIST:

❑ Fill one balloon with helium and tie a ribbon on it. (Use within 24 hours.) Inflate an identical balloon with regular air, just before class, so you can make the balloons as close to the same size as possible. Tie a matching ribbon to this balloon. Do not let students notice that one is helium filled and one is not.

 THE LESSON

Introduction: The world has known many holy men and religious leaders. **What are some of their names?** Buddha, Mohammed, Confucius, Moses. **How were these men different from Jesus?** Only Jesus claimed to be equal with God. **Was he? Is Jesus really God?** Today we will learn one reason to believe Jesus is God.

Demonstration: Show the balloons. Hold them tightly on the bottom, so no one can tell that one has helium and one does not. Invite the students to carefully observe the balloons. Notice the size, shape, color, and texture of the balloons. **Are there any differences between the two balloons?** So far, the balloons do not seem very different from each other. Now let the balloons go. **What differences do you notice?** One balloon floats to the ceiling. The other sinks to the ground.

Discussion: **How are these balloons like Jesus, compared to other religious leaders?** We can read about all these men in an encyclopedia. Each of them died and was buried, except Jesus. Jesus died, was buried and then rose from the dead. He did not die again. He is alive. His resurrection showed God's power. **What other things did Jesus do that no human could have ever done?** Some examples: changed the weather, loved people who were unlovable, multiplied food, healed people and raised them from the dead. Jesus is God, and we can know by looking at what he did. There is no human – past, present or future – who will match the incredible qualities of Jesus! He is above all, as the helium balloon is far above the other.

Application: **Whom will you serve?** Since Jesus is really God, he is the only one worth following. Other religions do not honor Jesus as God. They cannot lead us to know God forever. Only Jesus can.

Something Extra: Find an encyclopedia or visit the Internet. Read entries for Mohammed, Buddha and Confucius. Even read the entry for Moses. **Did any of these come back to life? Did any claim to be God?** Only Jesus made that claim.

Ideas for Use Anywhere

❑ Helium balloons are not available in some areas.

❑ Possible substitution: Wrap two gifts to look the same. One has a treasure or cross inside representing Jesus, and the other has names of religious leaders who have passed away.

❑ Teachers should research other leaders for students who do not have access to encyclopedias or the Internet.

BIBLE STORY IDEAS

THE TRANSFIGURATION (Mark 9:2-13)
Jesus took three disciples with him to a mountain. There, he showed his true glory to them. They were amazed. He is really God.

DOUBTING THOMAS (John 20:24-29)
Thomas did not believe. He thought Jesus was a great leader and prophet. But when he saw Jesus alive again, he learned that Jesus is God.

Did Jesus really come back from the dead?

The Answer

Yes! We can know Jesus came back from the dead because many witnesses saw him.

Bible Proof

●●●**1 CORINTHIANS 15:3b-6a -** ... Christ died for our sins ... was buried ... was raised on the third day according to the Scriptures, and ... he appeared to Peter, and then to the Twelve. After that, he appeared to more than five hundred of the brothers at the same time.

●●●**2 PETER 1:16 -** We did not follow cleverly invented stories when we told you about the power and coming of our Lord Jesus Christ, but we were eyewitnesses of his majesty.

Lesson Aim

To show that just as eyewitnesses share believable truth about cookies in a taste test, witnesses shared believable truth about Jesus' resurrection.

Before you teach ...

Though we cannot physically see Jesus and know from our own experience that he rose from the dead, we can know that he did so because of the witnesses who saw him. These witnesses recorded their encounters with the risen Lord in the Bible. They risked their lives to tell the truth about his resurrection. Their story is true!

Materials

❑ at least three different types of cookies (It would be great if the prettiest ones were stale!)

❑ several small paper plates

❑ OPTIONAL: one cookie for each student

TO DO LIST:

❑ Set up several small plates, each with a different kind of cookie. Cover and place off to the side (otherwise, hungry students may sneak off with your lesson).

THE LESSON

Introduction: **How many of you believe that Christopher Columbus discovered America? How do you know he did?** People have written about him in historical records. **How many of you believe Jesus rose from the dead? Can we really know?** This cookie test will help us think about Jesus.

Demonstration: Display the plates of cookies. Ask for two witnesses to help with a cookie test. Ask witness #1 which cookie is the best, but do not let him touch or eat any of them! Listen to his or her recommendation. Next, ask witness #2 which cookie is best. Instruct #2 to touch, smell, taste (or whatever else) in order to determine accurately which is the best. After the students finish, ask witness #2 to tell you which cookie is best. Then, ask the rest of the class which witness they believe more. **Why?** One student spent time with the cookies and investigated them thoroughly. He would know the truth. The other witness did not really experience the cookies.

Discussion: **What does this teach us about the importance of witnesses?** Without them, we are uncertain about what to believe. It is always best to have more than one witness, since everyone may have a slightly different viewpoint. Read 1 Corinthians 15:3-6. **Who saw Jesus alive? Had these people spent any time with Jesus?** Yes! They observed Jesus both before and after the crucifixion; therefore, they would know whether or not it was really Jesus. They saw him eat, they touched him, and they heard him speak. **How many people saw Jesus alive?** A lot. The disciples did not make up this story. They risked their lives to tell the truth. Some were even executed for doing so. **Would you die for a lie?**

Application: **Do you believe Jesus came back to life?** This one truth changed the disciples' lives! **How can it change your life?** Challenge your students to tell someone about Jesus this week. Tell them why they can know Jesus is alive.

Ideas for Use Anywhere

❑ Instead of cookies, offer fruit or candies. It is not necessary to have one for every student if this is not available as a treat.

❑ Instead of referring to Christopher Columbus, choose a locally famous explorer or hero.

Something Extra: Make a batch of cookies. Share them with a friend. Find out whether they believe Jesus came back from the dead.

BIBLE STORY IDEAS

GREAT COMMISSION & ASCENSION (Matthew 28:16-20; Acts 1:1-11) Jesus not only met with the disciples, but he also told them to be witnesses of his resurrection to all people of the world. He is really alive!

THE RESURRECTION (Matthew 28:1-15)
Many people saw Jesus alive: women, disciples and others. He really rose from the dead.

Can Jesus really be God and man at the same time?

Materials

☐ a diamond ring or piece of jewelry on a plate or tray

☐ washable, gooey stuff (ketchup, mustard, mud)

☐ damp paper towels or cloth

The Answer

Yes! Jesus demonstrated all of the attributes of God while fully experiencing a human life. He is really God and man.

Bible Proof

●●● **JOHN 1:14 -** The Word became flesh and made his dwelling among us. We have seen his glory, the glory of the One and Only, who came from the Father, full of grace and truth.

●●● **HEBREWS 1:3 -** The Son is the radiance of God's glory and the exact representation of his being ...

Lesson Aim

To show that a diamond ring covered with ordinary stuff is still precious, just as Jesus, in an ordinary human body, was still God.

Before you teach ...

It does not seem that Jesus could be both God and man at the same time, but he is. According to the Bible, God chose to reveal himself to us through Christ, displaying his humble, gentle love for us. It was a great act of restraint and humility for God to do this. But he did it. He was both God and man. He understands our weaknesses. He has power to help us. What a wonderful encouragement.

TO DO LIST:

☐ There are no special preparations.

☐ Tell a personal story about how Jesus' perfect example has inspired you.

76

 # THE LESSON

Introduction: **Can Jesus really be God and man at the same time? Why do you think so?** Ask for several student volunteers to help you try to understand the answer.

Demonstration: Show the ring. Ask students to describe it. Discuss its value, in both monetary terms and relationship terms. Place the ring in the center of the pie plate. Invite each volunteer to dump or squeeze a different type of gooey substance onto the ring. After each addition ask, **"Is the wedding ring still a valuable wedding ring?"** Yes! Finally, clean the ring with paper towels.

Discussion: **How is this diamond ring like Jesus?** He has all the power of God in him (God's Son), but he came to earth and allowed himself to take on a very ordinary human body. Unlike God, our bodies get sick, they get tired, they do not always work right. They eventually all die. Even though Jesus put himself into this ordinary situation, he was still special underneath. He was still God's Son. He was both God and man. **Do you think it was easy for Jesus to live in an ordinary body? To have ordinary parents? To live in an ordinary house?** He restrained his powers to live as a human. He was really God and a man at the same time.

Application: Invite a student to read Hebrews 1:3. **How important is it that Jesus is God? What can he do because he has all of God's power in him? How important is it that Jesus was a man? Can he understand us? Does he know what it is like to live in an ordinary body? How can this help us?** Jesus became a man, lived a perfect life as an example to us, and also became the only person worthy to pay the price for our sins to be forgiven forever. **Do you believe in Jesus Christ, God and man?**

Ideas for Use Anywhere

❑ If jewelry is not available, find something small that children would recognize as valuable – and that can be cleaned after the demonstration.

❑ Or, cover the jewelry item with layers that are not as messy, such as a cloth, a box, a cup, a hat, etc.

Something Extra: Read Hebrews 4:14-16 in a simple Bible version. **How does it help us to know that Jesus experienced real human temptation? In what way does his example help us?** We know he understands. We can pray to him for help when we feel weak and tempted.

BIBLE STORY IDEAS

TRANSFIGURATION (Mark 9:2-8)
Jesus revealed his true nature to three of his disciples. He was God and man, choosing to live as a humble servant while on earth.

CALMING OF THE STORM (Matthew 8:23-27)
Jesus surprised his disciples. This miracle showed them that he was more than a man – he was God!

PART 6

Questions about God and Me

Why did God make me?

Materials

- ❑ tub of garden dirt or potting soil
- ❑ a bucket of water
- ❑ soap and towels

The Answer

God made us so that we could know him and bring him glory.

Bible Proof

● ● ●**EPHESIANS 2:10 -** For we are God's workmanship, created in Christ Jesus to do good works, which God prepared in advance for us to do.

● ● ●**ROMANS 8:29a -** For those God foreknew he also predestined to be conformed to the likeness of his Son.

Lesson Aim

To show that though God crafted us from ordinary materials, like dirt, he made us for extraordinary things, to know him and to bring him glory.

Before you teach ...

God spoke all creation into being. From the beginning, though, man was special. God did a "hands on" work. He crafted people, creating them to be up close and personal right from the start. Relationship. It's exactly why God made us. This lesson will help your students see God's plan for them and recognize the incredible privilege they have of knowing the God of the universe and serving him.

TO DO LIST:

- ❑ Gather materials.
- ❑ Cover demonstration area with a towel or newspaper.

 THE LESSON

Introduction: Ask your students whether they have ever wondered why God made them. He could have only made animals or beautiful planets. He could have stopped with the angels. **Why did he make people?**

Demonstration: Invite three volunteers who do not mind getting a little dirty to help with this demonstration. Give volunteers several minutes to moisten the dirt and work with it, trying to form the shape of a person or an animal. **Can it be done?** Now try bringing the creation to life. **Can you breathe on it and bring it to life?** No. Thank the volunteers and let them clean their hands with water, soap and towels.

Discussion: Scientists tell us that all living things are made with materials as ordinary as dirt, water and the invisible chemicals found in the air. **Could you make life from this recipe?** No, neither can scientists. But God used these ordinary ingredients to create people. All of his other creations he simply spoke into being. People, he handcrafted. **Why did he make us?** He did not make us to be ordinary. He made us to have relationship with him. All other creations simply obey God's command without choosing. People, on the other hand, must choose whether they want to know him and follow him. When people ignore God, they miss out on the most important friendship in their lives. They do not bring glory to God.

Application: If God made us so that we could know him, we are not ordinary like dirt! God made each person special. **Have you begun a relationship with your Creator? Have you asked him to be part of your life?** Invite any students who have not already done so to receive Christ, now. **If you have started a friendship with God, what are you doing to grow closer to him?** These things help us grow a great relationship with God: pray each day, read or learn about him from the Bible, and go to church or Sunday School. **What will you do this week?**

Something Extra: Have you wondered how you can honor and serve God? Grow your relationship with him by working together with God. Pray and consider one new way God wants each child to serve or honor him in the coming week. Do it!

Ideas for Use Anywhere

☐ Students may not be familiar with science concepts. Emphasize the creativity (and limitations) of an artist or gardener.

BIBLE STORY IDEAS

YOUNG DAVID CHOSEN BY GOD (1 Samuel 16, Psalm 139, Psalm 23)
David knew he was formed by God. He knew his life had purpose from the beginning. He was made to know and love God as his Shepherd.

GOD SEES HAGAR AND ISHMAEL (Genesis 16)
God created all people. He had a plan for Hagar and Ishmael. He blessed them as they reached out in relationship to him.

Why didn't God make me as cool as my friends?

Materials

☐ a variety of cups and glasses (old, new, chipped, polished)

☐ a pitcher of water

The Answer

God made each of us unique, but we were all made to do good things.

Bible Proof

●●● **EPHESIANS 2:10 -** For we are God's workmanship, created in Christ Jesus to do good works, which God prepared in advance for us to do.

●●● **ROMANS 12:4-5a -** Just as each of us has one body with many members, and these members do not all have the same function, so in Christ we who are many form one body ...

●●● **ROMANS 9:20b-21 -** Shall what is formed say to him who formed it, "Why did you make me like this?" Does not the potter have the right to make out of the same lump of clay some pottery for noble purposes and some for common use?

Lesson Aim

To show that just as different kinds of cups and glasses are made to be filled with water, different kinds of people are all made to do good things, through Christ.

Before you teach ...

Comparison. Kids do to it all the time. They notice differences in clothing, abilities, appearance and status. Kids want to fit in but also to be special. This lesson teaches how God planned to fill both these desires.

TO DO LIST:

☐ Pray for your students to have godly peer influences.

☐ There are no other special preparations.

? THE LESSON

Introduction: **How many of you have cool friends? What do you think is great about them? How are you different from your friends? Do you ever wish you could be more like someone else?** It is very tempting to compare ourselves, to think that we are not as good as someone else. Today's "serious" experiment will help us understand that this is not God's plan for us at all.

Demonstration: Line up the cups, mugs and glasses on a table visible to all students. Ask for volunteers to help with this experiment. The goal of the test is to see which of these containers is capable of holding water. Invite one student at a time to pour water into any empty cup or glass. Act surprised each time it works. Applaud the volunteers. **Did all the cups hold water? Are you surprised?** No. All cups and glasses were meant to hold water, no matter what their size or shape. Though they look different, they are all equally useful. They are all just as capable of holding the precious water.

Discussion: These cups remind us of how God sees us. Drinking glasses were made to hold water. **What were we made for?** To know Christ, first, but also to do good works. To begin with, every person was made with the ability to have a relationship with God, just as all cups hold water. Read Romans 12:4-5 and Romans 9:20b-21. God also notices our differences; in fact, he is responsible for those differences. Every person was made with unique gifts and abilities to use to serve the Kingdom of God. **Will we all look the same as we serve Jesus?** No. Every person is different. Every person is needed. Now that's cool!

Application: **Have you compared yourself to others and thought you were not good enough to follow Jesus? What good works did God create for you to do that others might not think of? What can you do in the coming week to serve Jesus better?**

Something Extra: Invite students to think of a person who needs to be cheered up. Bring him or her a cup with milk – and cookies. Visit with them. Afterward, thank God for the chance to do something good for others.

Ideas for Use Anywhere

❑ Milk and cookies are a North American treat. Substitute juice or water, and crackers or fruit. Find out what is available and enjoyed locally.

BIBLE STORY IDEA

ALL PARTS OF THE BODY ARE IMPORTANT (Romans 12) Paul taught the church that everyone in the body of Christ has a job to do. All jobs are not the same, neither are all people. God designed it that way. Every unique person is important to God.

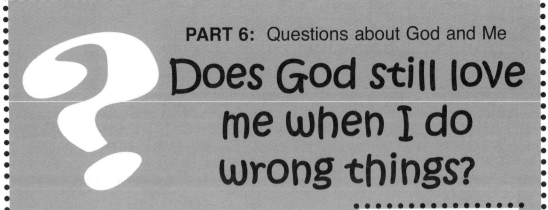

Does God still love me when I do wrong things?

Materials

❑ the ground

The Answer

Yes! No matter what we do, we cannot be separated from God's love. He hates the sin and wants us to repent, but he always loves us.

Bible Proof

●●● **ROMANS 8:38-39 -** … (Nothing) … will be able to separate us from the love of God that is in Christ Jesus our Lord.

●●● **ROMANS 5:8 -** But God demonstrates his own love for us in this: While we were still sinners, Christ died for us.

●●● **1 JOHN 1:9 -** If we confess our sins, he is faithful and just and will forgive us our sins and purify us from all unrighteousness.

Lesson Aim

To show that just as the earth cannot be shaken, no matter what we do, God's love is constant, no matter what we do.

Before you teach ...

Consistency. Few kids experience it, especially in this rapidly changing world. Best friends move, grandparents get sick or die, families reorganize and technology advances all the time. Kids need to know that God does not change. Though God despises sin, God's love for each of your students is a forever thing. One of the most consistent truths about God is that he loves us no matter what.

TO DO LIST:

❑ There are no special preparations.

❑ Welcome your students to class by name.

 # THE LESSON

Introduction: **Do your friends like you? All the time? What if you do something wrong to hurt their feelings?** We can be angry with our friends when they do wrong things. They can be angry with us. Sometimes the feelings last for a long time. **What about God? Does he get angry? Does he still love us when we do wrong things?**

Demonstration: Invite your students to help you with a "tricky" experiment. Choose several student volunteers. Ask the rest to help observe the facts. What we need to know is, **"Can the planet earth be shaken?"** Ask each volunteer to try something different to shake the earth. Have one stand on his head, one jump up and down, one shout, one do a somersault, one do a twirling jump, etc. After each demonstration ask the kids if the earth is rocking. Add up the score. **How many times did the earth shake? Could we move the earth out of its orbit around the sun?**

Discussion: This experiment reminds us of an important truth about God's love. Invite a student to read Romans 8:38-39. **According to the verse, what kinds of things can separate us from God's love?** Nothing! **How is God's love like the earth?** We cannot shake it. It is always there no matter what. Ask again. **Does God still love you when you do wrong things?**

Application: Just like it hurts when our friends do not want to talk with us, God is sad when we do not talk with him. Even if we have done something wrong, he wants the relationship to be healed. He wants us to talk with him about it and get forgiveness. He wants us to stop doing wrong things and grow an even better relationship with him. **Do you need to talk to God today?** Pray silently, privately, to God. Ask for forgiveness for any wrong things.

Something Extra: Go for a walk. Challenge your students to count the number of steps they take on the walk. **Do their steps shake the earth? Does God still love them when they do wrong things?**

Ideas for Use Anywhere

❑ In developing areas science concepts such as "orbit" or "planets" may be unfamiliar. Instead, focus on trying to shake the ground itself.

BIBLE STORY IDEAS

JACOB GETS A SECOND CHANCE (Genesis 27 & 28:10-17)
Jacob was a deceiver. He did many wrong things. But God had a plan for his life. God showed his love to Jacob, helping him and blessing him.

MOSES (Exodus 2-3)
Moses killed a man. Nevertheless, God called Moses to deliver his people. God accepted no excuses from Moses. However, God's love for Moses prevailed.

How do I know God loves me?

Materials

❑ masking tape

❑ 10-12 foot "red carpet" (a towel, cloth, blanket, or red poster paper)

The Answer

God's Word says he loves us. He made a way for us to be close with him forever through Jesus.

Bible Proof

●●●**ROMANS 5:8 -** But God demonstrates his own love for us in this: While we were still sinners, Christ died for us.

●●●**1 JOHN 4:9 -** This is how God showed his love among us: He sent his one and only Son into the world that we might live through him.

Lesson Aim

To discuss how God showed his great love for us by sending Jesus to pay the price to give us a "red carpet" welcome into God's presence, now and for eternity.

Before you teach ...

How do we know when someone cares for us? We might know by what they say. But even more, their actions demonstrate how they feel about us. Christ's action for us was the most incredible demonstration of love, ever. He gave his life to make a way for us to come into God's presence. He has rolled the red carpet out for each of us! Let your students know, today, how much he cares for them.

TO DO LIST:

❑ Place two 3-foot strips of masking tape on the floor, 10-12 feet apart, parallel to each other. Have the "red carpet" rolled up and ready off to one side.

86

? THE LESSON

Introduction: Ask your students how they know when someone really cares about them. **Have you ever known someone who said they cared about you only to have them do something really hurtful to you later?** When someone really cares about us, their actions match their words. **Do you think God really cares about you? How can we know?**

Demonstration: Ask for a volunteer who is good at sports. Ask this person to stand with toes on one line of the tape and try to jump to the other line without touching the floor between. Let several others try, also. **Can anyone do it?** No. It is too far. Next, roll out the red carpet between the two pieces of tape. **Can you cross from one line to the other without touching the floor covering?** Try again. It's easy, now, because there is a path, a bridge.

Discussion: **How does this demonstration remind us of God's care for us?** No matter how hard we try, we cannot get close to God on our own. Our sin keeps us separated from God. When Jesus died on the cross, he paid for our sin to be forgiven and made a way, like this carpet, for people to get to God and have eternal life. We could not do it for ourselves; it is a gift from God. Ask your students if they have ever heard of "rolling out the red carpet"? Hotels or restaurants use this to welcome special visitors, like the President or king. It shows respect for people and welcomes them in a very fancy style. This is how God feels about us! He rolls out the red carpet.

Application: **Have you responded to God's invitation to receive his love? Have you received Christ as your Savior?** Thank God, together, for loving us so much. **How can you show your love back to God?**

Ideas for Use Anywhere

❑ The "red carpet" concept may not be familiar in some cultures. Focus on the concept of Jesus being a bridge instead.

❑ If red cloth is not available, substitute another cloth, rope, string, tape or a wooden board to create a bridge.

Something Extra: Invite students to design a board game or maze. The object of the game is to get to heaven, but there is only one way to get there: across the red carpet called "Jesus' blood." Play the game to remember what Jesus did.

BIBLE STORY IDEAS

THE NARROW & WIDE GATES (Matthew 7:13-14)
Jesus taught that the way to God was narrow. Those who find their way to God through belief in Jesus will have eternal life.

PARABLE OF THE LOST SHEEP (Luke 15:1-7)
God truly loves us as a shepherd. He does not want us to be lost. He wants us with him now and forever.

Why can't I hear God talk?

Materials

❑ a radio

❑ an outlet for plugging in the radio (or batteries)

The Answer

Though God does not speak as humans speak to each other, we can still hear God's voice if we are "tuned in" to him through his Word.

Bible Proof

●●●**REVELATION 3:20 -** Here I am! I stand at the door and knock. If anyone hears my voice and opens the door, I will come in and eat with him, and he with me.

●●●**JOHN 10:27 -** My sheep listen to my voice; I know them, and they follow me.

●●●**JOHN 16:13 -** But when he, the Spirit of truth, comes, he will guide you into all truth. He will not speak on his own; he will speak only what he hears, and he will tell you what is yet to come.

Lesson Aim

To show that just as we cannot hear the radio if it is not tuned into a channel, we cannot hear God's voice unless we are tuned in to his Word.

Before you teach ...

It bothers kids. Why can't they hear God talk? Some may question his existence because of this silence. Others may not understand how to obey God when they cannot hear him. It is not as mysterious as some would make it seem. Kids learn God's words from the Bible, just like adults. God's Holy Spirit reminds them of his words, as needed, deep in their hearts. Kids can learn to recognize his voice and obey. Their faith will grow by leaps and bounds as they do.

TO DO LIST:

❑ Gather materials.

❑ Check to be sure radio reception works in your teaching setting.

88

? THE LESSON

Introduction: **How many of you had a conversation with your parents or siblings this morning? Could you hear them talk? How many of you prayed to God today? Could you hear God talk to you? Why or why not?**

Demonstration: Show the radio to your students. Ask them simple questions about the radio, guiding them to explain that it can give warning messages, news, music, stories. Try listening to some music. Place the radio next to your ear without turning it on. **I don't hear anything, do you?** It does not work. There is no music. Act disgusted, ready to walk away. Let your students discover that it needs to be plugged in and turned on. After fixing the problem, notice that the radio works, but have the station turned to news. Explain that you wanted to listen to music. Let a student help you find a music station.

Discussion: Tell your students the radio reminds you about why many people do not hear God's voice. There are some things people must do in order to hear God. They must "tune in" to his voice. **How do we "tune in" to God?** First, we must begin a relationship with him. When we do, God's Holy Spirit comes to live in us and with us always. Then, we need to tune in to God by reading from the Bible and praying. As we are ready and listening, the Holy Spirit reminds us of God's words as we need them. This is how we begin to hear God speak to us in our lives. It is very quiet. It is very real. It is how our friendship with God grows.

Ideas for "tuning in" to God

1. Read the Bible
2. Pray to God
3. Look and listen for his answers
4. Obey God's Word

Application: **Do you spend time in prayer and in God's Word?** This helps us hear God through his Spirit and his Word.

Ideas for Use Anywhere

❑Radios are available in most parts of the world. Some run on batteries rather than electricity. Adjust your lesson to refer to whichever power source is available.

Something Extra: Invite students to write down (or memorize) the ideas above. Let kids choose one specific thing they can do in the coming week in their own lives.

BIBLE STORY IDEA

JONAH IGNORES GOD (Jonah 1)
Jonah knew what God said. He refused to obey. When we obey, we can more easily hear God speak to us.

Why doesn't God give me what I ask for?

Materials

☐ a kid's search book ("Where's Waldo®" or "I Spy®"?)

The Answer

God gives us what he knows is best for us according to his will, not ours.

Bible Proof

●●● **JAMES 4:3 -** When you ask, you do not receive, because you ask with wrong motives, that you may spend what you get on your pleasures.

●●● **ROMANS 8:28 -** And we know that in all things God works for the good of those who love him, who have been called according to his purpose.

Lesson Aim

To discuss that God sees everything that happens on our busy planet, and he knows how best to answer every person's prayer.

Before you teach ...

Especially in North America, kids think that if God really loves them, they should have everything they want, and life should be easy all the time. But it is not so. God does not answer our every wish every time we pray.

God knows exactly what we need. He even knows that troubles and hardship can bring about the most amazing growth in us. He is not afraid to answer kids' — and adults'— prayers by giving what is best for them ... according to his will, not ours.

TO DO LIST:

☐ Find a search book by checking with older kids in your class, or by visiting a library.

☐ Pray for your students to understand.

 **THE LESSON**

Introduction: **Have you ever asked God for something you really wanted and then not received it? What happened?** If God loves to give good gifts to his children, it seems that he would answer all our prayers for good things. **Right?**

Demonstration: Invite one or two students to take turns finding the main search character or other hidden objects in the pictures. **Why are some hard to find? Why are some easy to find? How long would it take to find all the hidden items?** It might take quite a while because the pictures are so busy and crazy that objects are not easy to see right away.

Discussion: **What does God see when he looks down from heaven?** He sees billions of people doing billions of things in millions of different places, all with different personalities, different families, different needs, and different troubles. **Is it hard for God to see people and help them in this chaos?** Not at all. He can see every person, including kids, and counts the hairs on their head. **Is this something he would even NEED to know?** No, but he knows it all anyway. He knows the words we are going to say before we speak. **Then, why doesn't he give us what we ask for?** God knows what is best for us. He loves us too much to give us what we ask for all the time. When one person prays for rain and another prays for a sunny day, he knows what is really needed. He answers in the way that is best. **What would happen if we all got everything we wanted?** Selfish chaos.

Application: Invite a student to read Psalm 121:7-8. **Does God watch over us to spy on us? What is he watching for? How does he know how to best answer our prayers?** God sees everything and knows what is best. He wants the very best for us. Sometimes we do not ask for those things that are best for our lives.

Ideas for Use Anywhere

❏ Colors representing stop, wait and go will not have the same significance in all parts of the world (no traffic lights).

❏ Kids' search books may not be available. Invite students to find items on a crowded newspaper or magazine page, or hide items in your classroom.

Something Extra: Invite students to keep an unusual "Answer to Prayer" journal for two weeks. Give each a large piece of blank paper, a red paper circle, a green circle, and a yellow circle. Write prayer requests on the white paper. Write answers on the others. Record "yes" answers on the green paper, "no" answers on the red paper, and "wait" answers on the yellow. **Did God answer your prayers?**

BIBLE STORY IDEAS

PAUL'S "THORN" (2 Corinthians 12:9-10)
Paul prayed for God to remove his "thorn in the flesh." But God did not take it away.

DAVID'S SON DIES (2 Samuel 12:13-23)
David prayed for his son to live, but he still died.

PART 7

Questions about God and Eternity

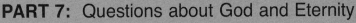

How long will I live?

Materials

☐ a new roll of bathroom tissue

The Answer

With Jesus as our Savior, we will live forever!

Bible Proof

●●● **1 JOHN 5:11-13 -** And this is the testimony: God has given us eternal life, and this life is in his Son. He who has the Son has life; he who does not have the Son of God does not have life. I write these things to you who believe in the name of the Son of God so that you may know that you have eternal life.

●●● **REVELATION 11:15b -** And there were loud voices in heaven, which said: "The kingdom of the world has become the kingdom of our Lord and of his Christ, and he will reign for ever and ever."

Lesson Aim

To show that just as one square of bathroom tissue is small compared to the whole roll, our life here on earth is just a small part of the eternal life God gives to those who believe in him.

Before you teach ...

We all would like to know how long we are going to live. The truth is our life here on earth is just a small part of our entire life if we have Jesus living in us. We get to spend eternity living in a much better place. Celebrate with your students today as you see a glimmer of the abundant and eternal life that God has planned for his children.

TO DO LIST:

☐ Gather materials.

☐ Prepare to tell the story of how you received Jesus as your Savior.

 **THE LESSON**

Introduction: **How old is the oldest person you know? How long will that person live? How long do you think you will live?** God has something even longer in mind for your students: forever. **How long is forever?** Invite students to participate in this demonstration to help them understand.

Demonstration: Give each student one square of bathroom tissue. Pretend that one square represents their life. Briefly discuss different stages of life from birth to old age, and show them where each might be on their tissue piece, as if it were a timeline. Together, consider enjoying a nice, long, full, fun life. Now, ask a student to read 1 John 5:13. Discuss the meanings of "eternal life." **How long is eternity?** Let kids help you unroll the bathroom tissue to the end of the roll. Go down hallways and stairs, out the door, around the building, etc. Help kids see how REALLY long it is.

Discussion: When it is all rolled out, remind students that this represents just the BEGINNING of eternity. It will go on forever. It begins here, on earth, when we receive Jesus as our Savior and start growing a friendship with him, but it goes on forever in heaven. There, we will rule with him, we will worship him, we will be with others who love and worship God. Heaven will be a wonderful place.

Application: **Do you have the Son? Have you received Jesus as your Savior?** Invite students who have never accepted Jesus as their Savior to do so. For others, stop and thank God for the gift of eternal life, given to us through Jesus.

Something Extra: Invite students to carry the square of bathroom tissue with them all week. Keep it in a pocket. Every time they notice it, challenge students to thank God for the gift of eternal life God gave them through Jesus.

Ideas for Use Anywhere

❑ Rolls of toilet tissue may not be readily available in all areas. Use a ball of string or yarn instead. Students may each receive a piece of string to tie around their finger.

❑ Avoid throwing away the string or yarn, as this will seem wasteful in many cultures.

BIBLE STORY IDEAS

JESUS TEACHES NICODEMUS THE WAY (John 3)
Nicodemus learned about being born again and receiving eternal life.

RICH YOUNG RULER (Mark 10:17-31)
The rich young ruler had questions about eternal life.

Do animals go to heaven?

Materials

- ☐ a bicycle
- ☐ one or two small pets (fish, hamster, turtle)

The Answer

We don't know. The Bible teaches that God made heaven for himself and people. Other creatures are mentioned in heaven, but we do not know how many will be there.

Bible Proof

- ●●●**GENESIS 1:27 -** So God created man in his own image, in the image of God he created him, male and female he created them.
- ●●●**ISAIAH 11:6 -** The wolf will live with the lamb, the leopard will lie down with the goat, the calf and the lion and the yearling together; and a little child will lead them.
- ●●●**REVELATION 21:3-4 -** And I heard a loud voice from the throne saying, "Now the dwelling of God is with men, and he will live with them. They will be his people, and God himself will be with them and be their God. He will wipe every tear from their eyes. There will be no more death or mourning or crying or pain, for the old order of things has passed away."

Lesson Aim

To show that just as bicycles were not made for animals to ride, heaven was not created for animals, but for people and their God.

Before you teach ...

Modern kids are taught to respect the environment. In fact, many have come to believe that animals are as valuable – or even more so – than people. In addition, kids love their pets. They want to be friends forever. Certainly, God made animals for us to enjoy, and we must respect and care for this earth. But God made people in his image, to be the guests of honor with him in heaven, forever.

TO DO LIST:

- ☐ Pray for your students.

?: THE LESSON

Introduction: **How many of you have pets? What are their names? What can your pets do?** Enjoy hearing about your students' pets for several minutes. Give everyone a chance to speak, if possible. **What happens to your pets when they die? Do they go to heaven, like people (who believe in Jesus)?**

Demonstration: Show students the bicycle. Invite one or two to demonstrate how it works. Let them ride in a hallway or simply sit on the seat, then discuss how kids ride a bike. Next, show the animals you brought (or pictures). Try to help one or two animals ride the bicycle (or imagine this). Enjoy the resulting comedy. **Can animals ride a bicycle? Are bicycles made for animals to ride?** No!

Discussion: Explain that the bicycle teaches us a truth about animals and heaven. Bicycles were made for people to ride, not for animals. (A few circus animals may have learned to ride trick bicycles, but they are not common.) In the same way, heaven was made for God and his people, not for animals. People and animals are not the same. Genesis tells us that people alone were created in God's image. Read Revelation 21:3-4. **Are pets mentioned in heaven?** Some verses, talking about a time when God's people reign with him, mention animals living together peacefully, like a lion living with a lamb. We do not know if this will take place in heaven. In heaven, though, there will be no more tears. Even if we do not see our animals, we will not be sad. Jesus will be there. We can enjoy him more than we would any animal friend (or any other person) we now know on earth.

Application: **Are you friends with God? Have you received Jesus as your Savior?** Every person (not animal) is invited to be forgiven of their sin and receive Christ. He is the very best friend a kid can have – far better than any pets we love.

Ideas for Use Anywhere

❑ Draw pictures if real animals are not available.

❑ In many parts of the world, people do not keep animals as pets. Adjust by discussing "animals" (chickens, goats or cows) instead of "pets".

Something Extra: Let your students imagine their pets could learn the truth about Jesus. Invite students to practice telling friends about Jesus, using their pets. Pets can be so easy to talk to!

BIBLE STORY IDEAS

DESCRIPTION OF HEAVEN (Revelation 7, 21)
Heaven will be a beautiful place filled with people who know and love God.

CHARIOTS OF FIRE (2 Kings 2:1-12)
Elijah went up to heaven in a fiery whirlwind that Elisha described as "the chariots and horsemen of Israel." Will there be horses in heaven? Will they be fiery? We do not know.

What will I look like in heaven?

Materials

❏ popcorn

❏ an air popper

The Answer

We get a new body that will be even better than what we have now!

Bible Proof

●●●**PHILIPPIANS 3:20-21 -** But our citizenship is in heaven. And we eagerly await a Savior from there, the Lord Jesus Christ who … will transform our lowly bodies so that they will be like his glorious body.

●●●**1 CORINTHIANS 15:51-52 -** Listen, I tell you a mystery: We will not all sleep, but we will all be changed – in a flash, in the twinkling of an eye, at the last trumpet. For the trumpet will sound, the dead will be raised imperishable, and we will be changed.

Lesson Aim

To show that just as a popcorn seed turns into something even better – in a flash, when we go to heaven, we will receive a new body that is better than our old one – in just a flash.

Before you teach ...

Kids fear the unknown. Heaven is definitely an unknown. People do not regularly return from heaven to tell us what it is like. No one has brought us a vacation brochure so that we are sure we even want to go there. But God has told us bits and pieces of what to expect, in his Word. One thing we know is that we will have new, wonderful bodies.

TO DO LIST:

❏ Gather materials.

98

? THE LESSON

Introduction: Invite students to study their hands, arms, etc. Notice differences they have from their friends. **What do you think you will look like in heaven?**

Demonstration: Show some popcorn. **What is this stuff?** These are actually dead seeds from a popcorn plant. **Do you like how these seeds look and feel? What could we do to make them even better?** Place seeds in the popper and wait. Watch them change, inside out, as they pop. **Do you like popcorn better as seeds or after it has been changed?** Enjoy tasting the popcorn together.

Discussion: This popcorn reminds us of a truth about ourselves and heaven. Read 1 Corinthians 15:51-52. **What will we be like in heaven? What is God going to do to our bodies?** He will transform our bodies and make them even better than what they are now! **How long will it take for our bodies to change?** In the twinkling of an eye. Just as we saw the kernels suddenly change into popped corn, we will be changed. We will not explode or be hurt in the process. Instead, we will receive a new body that will be glorious, like Jesus' heavenly body after he died and rose again. Our bodies will not experience pain. They will not get sick, grow old or die.

Application: **What else will be new in heaven?** Being close to Jesus, worshipping him, being together with loved ones. **What will be "old" in heaven?** Our friendship with Jesus does not need to be new. Every bit of effort we put into growing a close friendship with him, here and now, will be something we can enjoy and build upon in heaven. **What are you doing now to grow a closer friendship with Jesus?**

Ideas for Use Anywhere

❑Popcorn may not be available in all local areas.

❑If an air popper or microwave is not available, pop the corn using another method and bring it to class already popped. Show kernels before and after.

❑Students do not need to do "Something Extra" activity if supplies are not accessible.

Something Extra: Invite students to draw a picture of how they think they might look in their new bodies. Draw a picture of themselves as friends with Jesus. Mount these drawings on classroom walls.

BIBLE STORY IDEAS

TRANSFIGURATION (Matthew 17:1-9 or Mark 9:2-13) The disciples were allowed to see Jesus' glorified body. It was different. It was awesome. It will last forever, just like the body we will receive.

MAN HEALED AT THE POOL (John 5:1-15) Jesus is able to heal, fix and change bodies here on earth. Even more so, he will change our bodies to be brand new for eternity.

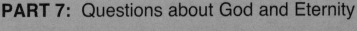

What will I need in heaven?

Materials

❑ a suitcase or bag

❑ items not needed in heaven: package of tissues, money, flashlight or candle, squirt gun, water bottle, bandages, medicine, picture of Jesus (optional)

The Answer

We will not need anything we have on earth. Everything we need will be there, and more.

Bible Proof

●●●**REVELATION 21:4 to 22:4** - He will wipe every tear from their eyes. There will be no more death or mourning or crying or pain … The foundation of the city walls were decorated with every kind of precious stone … The great street of the city was of pure gold … the glory of God gives it light, and the Lamb is its lamp … there will be no night there … nothing impure will ever enter it … the river of the water of life, as clear as crystal, flowing down the middle of the great street of the city … the leaves of the tree are for the healing of the nations … They will see his face.

Lesson Aim

To discuss how going to heaven will be different from going anywhere else in the world because we will not need to take anything there. God will supply it all.

Before you teach …

Heaven will be the most awesome place! Kids can't even begin to imagine its wonder. But kids can start to understand how complete heaven is by discovering what they WILL NOT need there. God will take care of our every need. It will be an incredible place.

TO DO LIST:

❑ Pack the suitcase or bag with items listed above.

 THE LESSON

Introduction: **How many of you have gone on a trip lately? Where did you go? What did you have to take? After you got there, did you realize you forgot something?** Maybe the weather was different than we imagined, or there was a game we could have played if we had brought the right equipment. We also need to prepare for the greatest trip of our lives … going to heaven. **Have you ever thought about what you will need in heaven?**

Demonstration: Open your suitcase and show the kids just exactly what you have already packed. Discuss whether you will need it in heaven or not. For each item ask, **"Will I need this?"** Unpack as you go. Let the kids help you discover that you will need nothing in your suitcase.

- ●**Package of Tissues -** There will not be sadness or pain, or tears to wipe away.
- ●**Money -** The streets are made of gold, and the foundation of the city is made out of jewels. We will not need any money or treasures.
- ●**Flashlight -** There will be light all day long. God will be the light.
- ●**Toy gun or knife -** There will not be anything impure. We will not need to defend ourselves from war or fighting.
- ●**Water bottle -** Where we are going, there is a river of life.
- ●**Bandages and Medicine -** Where we are going, there is a tree with leaves that heal every hurt or sickness.
- ●**Picture of Jesus -** We will not need a picture of Jesus. He will be with us.

What do we need to pack? Nothing in our suitcase! God has provided it all. The only thing we will need is something invisible: faith in Jesus Christ as our Savior.

Discussion: **How does it make you feel to have this incredible place to look forward to?** God has provided everything we need in heaven. All we need is faith in Jesus. Have a student read Ephesians 2:8-9. **Have you prepared for the trip by placing your faith in Jesus Christ?**

Application: Invite each student to name one thing they thank God for about heaven. Praise him together.

Ideas for Use Anywhere

❑ Substitute items that are locally available and have meaning for children in the community. Check with their leaders to be sure.

Something Extra: Invite students to work together to create a poster of heaven as they imagine it will be.

BIBLE STORY IDEA
DESCRIPTION OF HEAVEN (Revelation 22)
All are invited to come to heaven and live with God forever.

Will everyone go to heaven?

Materials

❑ a chair

The Answer

No. Only those who truly believe in Jesus Christ as their Lord and Savior will go to heaven.

Bible Proof

●●●**JOHN 14:6 -** Jesus answered, "I am the way and the truth and the life. No one comes to the Father except through me."

●●●**ROMANS 10:9-10 -** That if you confess with your mouth, "Jesus is Lord," and believe in your heart that God raised him from the dead, you will be saved. For it is with your heart that you believe and are justified, and it is with your mouth that you confess and are saved.

Lesson Aim

To show that true belief (the requirement to get to heaven) involves doing something tangible to show we believe.

Before you teach ...

"Just believe." It is a common saying in and out of the church. What are we to believe in? How do we know what to believe? How do we know that a person truly believes in anything? Regardless of the truth in question, true belief always results in action. Those who believe do something about it. Today's lesson teaches your students that no one can go to heaven without faith: faith that leads to action. Enjoy challenging your students to take steps to show they really believe in Jesus.

TO DO LIST:

❑ There are no special preparations.

❑ Tell your students the story of when you first believed in Christ for salvation.

102

 THE LESSON

Introduction: The Bible teaches us that only those who believe in Jesus will be able to go to heaven. Read John 3:16 to confirm this. **But what does it mean to believe? Can everyone do it? Is it hard?**

Demonstration: Ask for a very brave volunteer. Give this person a bravery test. Tell the student you need him or her to do something very courageous. You need the volunteer to sit in the chair. Just as he or she is about to sit, stop the demonstration. **Wait! Do you believe this chair will hold your weight? Are you really sure?** Invite the student to sit if he or she REALLY believes. When the student sits in the chair, act very impressed. Celebrate his or her courage. Thank the student for helping.

Discussion: **Were you impressed by our volunteer's bravery?** No. Your students will not have been impressed that the volunteer sat in a chair. **What did this demonstration teach us about "belief"?** When we believe something is true, we always do something about it. The volunteer believed the chair was strong enough to hold him/her, so the volunteer sat on it. Our actions show what is in our hearts. **Do we really believe in Jesus if we have not acted upon our belief?** Read Romans 10:9-10. **What does God require of us to get to heaven?** Belief and confession. **What if we do not believe?** We will not go to heaven.

Application: **How are you showing that you believe in Jesus? What are your actions telling other people?**

Something Extra: Challenge your students to a one week "Do I Believe?" game. Give each a small paper bracelet that says "Do I Believe?" Challenge students to ask themselves what they have done each day that shows they believe in him. Check back with your students next time you meet.

Ideas for Use Anywhere

❑ This demonstration should work anywhere around the world.

❑ Children can participate in the "Something Extra" activity without a paper bracelet, if school supplies are not readily available.

BIBLE STORY IDEAS

PARABLE OF THE SOWER (Luke 8:1-15)
Not everyone who hears the truth about God will be saved, only those who believe in God's Word about Jesus and obey.

THE PRISON GUARD BELIEVES (Acts 16:16-34)
Paul and Silas told the prison guard about Jesus. He believed and was saved.

Do bad people go to heaven?

Materials

☐ kids with arms!

The Answer

No, if they have not received Jesus. Yes, if they have. The same is true for "good" people. Everyone sins. Only those who believe in Jesus can receive eternal life.

Bible Proof

●●● **ROMANS 3:10b-12 -** There is no one righteous, not even one; there is no one who understands, no one who seeks God. All have turned away, they have together become worthless; there is no one who does good, not even one.

●●● **EPHESIANS 2:8-9 -** For it is by grace you have been saved, through faith – and this not from yourselves, it is the gift of God – not by works, so that no one can boast.

Lesson Aim

To show that just as kids cannot reach the ceiling on their own, no one, whether "good" or "bad," is good enough to get to God by his or her own good works.

Before you teach ...

Kids will usually be happy to agree that bad people should be punished. Unfortunately, the Bible teaches that even those who commit "small sins" are bad. They cannot enter heaven. The only way any of us can enter heaven is to receive forgiveness of our sin from Christ. It is a tough, hard lesson. But it leads to an amazing, forever life with God!

TO DO LIST:

☐ Pray for your students!

104

? THE LESSON

Introduction: **How many of you have seen a bad guy in a movie or in real life? Do you think bad people go to heaven? Why? Do good people go to heaven? Why do you think so?** Invite students to try an experiment with you to understand what the Bible says about it.

Demonstration: Invite all the students to lie on the floor on their backs. Next, instruct them to all touch the ceiling with their hands. Try. Try harder! If the ceiling is very high, students may even stand and try to jump to reach the ceiling. **Can anyone do it? Are some closer than others?** Some arms may be longer than others. **Who is the closest? Did that person actually reach the ceiling?** No.

Discussion: Have a student read Romans 3:10-12. **According to God, who is good enough to go to heaven?** No one! God says we are all "bad guys" because all of us have sinned and broken God's laws. **How is this like our experiment trying to touch the ceiling? Does it matter who is closest?** No. **How can anyone reach heaven, then?** Read Ephesians 2:8-9. God's grace (love) was shown to us when he sent Jesus to die on the cross and pay the price for our sin to be forgiven. If we ask him to forgive our sin, and have faith that he does, we can be saved. This is the only way we can receive eternal life. **Have you done this?**

Application: **Whom do you consider a bad guy? Did Jesus die for this person? Can he or she go to heaven?** Pray for people and kids your students know ("good" or "bad"), who have not believed in Jesus. Ask God to help them come to believe in him so they can go to heaven, too.

Ideas for Use Anywhere

☐ In many areas, it is not culturally acceptable to lie on the floor or ground. Instead, stand and try to reach the ceiling. Or, go outside and try to reach the clouds.

BIBLE STORY IDEAS

CRIMINAL SAVED ON THE CROSS (Luke 23:38-43)
Jesus forgave the criminal for his sin. Jesus died though he had no sin. He died to take our punishment for us.

PETER'S DENIAL (Luke 22:31-34; 54-62)
Peter let Jesus down when Jesus needed him most. He said he did not even know Christ. Jesus forgave him, not because he deserved it, but because he loved Peter and had paid the price for his sin to be forgiven forever.

Won't heaven be boring?

Materials

❑ a party planning chart (an erasable board or large piece of paper)

The Answer

No way! We will be close to Jesus forever in the most amazing place ever created.

Bible Proof

●●●**JOHN 14:2-3 -** In my Father's house are many rooms; if it were not so, I would have told you. I am going there to prepare a place for you. And if I go and prepare a place of you, I will come back and take you to be with me that you also may be where I am.
●●●**REVELATION 22:5 -** ... And they will reign for ever and ever.
●●●**HEBREWS 1:16a -** They were longing for a better country, a heavenly one.

Lesson Aim

To discuss how heaven will be better than any party we could ever plan because Jesus has been planning it for thousands of years.

Before you teach ...

Singing hymns. Flying around with little angel wings. White nothingness. Though this is often what comes to mind when kids consider heaven, it is not an accurate picture of our future home. Heaven will be an amazing, exciting, wonderful place. Although we do not know all the details, we know the one who does. Jesus is not boring at all. He has been working to plan this place for us for thousands of years. He created the earth in a few days. Just imagine what heaven will be like if he's spent that much time preparing it for us. Wow!

TO DO LIST:

❑ Pray for your students to understand and to enjoy anticipating a forever friendship with Jesus in heaven!

 # THE LESSON

Introduction: Invite your students to help you plan a fantastic party. Pretend that cost is not a problem. They can spend as much as they like.

Demonstration: Give as many students as possible a turn to answer some of the questions below. Write their answers on an erasable board or large paper.

> Where would you hold the party?
> What special guests would you invite?
> What food would you eat?
> What activities would you plan for your guests?
> What would you give as party favors?

Think about this party. **Would it be fun to attend?**

Discussion: **Have you ever wondered about heaven? What will we do in heaven for all those years of eternity?** There may not be television or video games. There will be no problems, no school. **Won't it be boring?** We may think that God and his rules will be there, but not much else. Invite a good reader to read Revelation 21. Instruct students to close their eyes while it is read. Imagine the beauty of it all. Jesus and the whole family of God will be there together. It will be like the best family reunion ever — where everyone loves each other and God. We will rule and reign with Christ.

Application: **Are you going to the best party ever planned? Do all your friends know about heaven? Have they heard about Jesus' plan for them to know him now and forever?** Invite your students to talk about heaven with at least one friend in the coming week. Share the truth about how "non-boring" heaven will be.

Ideas for Use Anywhere

❑ If paper or an erasable board is not available, plan the party in your imaginations. No need to write down ideas.

❑ Realize that different cultures will have VERY different ideas for celebrations. Listen carefully.

❑ For kids in poverty areas, simply having enough food, or a place to sleep will be highlights.

Something Extra: Plan a party with your students. Enjoy good food, fun and friends. Imagine how much more exciting God's forever celebration in heaven will be.

BIBLE STORY IDEA

PARABLE OF MINAS (Luke 19:11-27) Those who have been faithful in small things will be rewarded and given the opportunity to rule with Christ.

Bible Verse Index

Old Testament

New Testament

Bible Story Index

Old Testament

New Testament

For additional copies of
"Object Lessons Answering Kids' Toughest Questions about God"
or
"Object Lessons Answering Kids' Toughest Questions about Life"
or
other fresh resources for
reaching and discipling children

ANYWHERE!

around the world,
contact us at:

Kidzana
Ministries

8229 44th Avenue West (Suite G)
Mukilteo, WA 98275
425-353-8027
FAX: 425-954-4006
e-mail: info@kidzana.org

800-222-6241 (U.S. only)
www.kidzana.org

Visit

www.kidzana.org

to learn more about involving
yourself, your kids and your church
in reaching children around the world for Christ

OPERATION 1+1
A missions education and giving project for
kids. Complete with DVD, supplies,
activities, and fun ideas to involve your kids
in reaching kids for Christ.

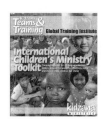

GLOBAL TRAINING INSTITUTE
Equip yourself, your staff or others in your
church or organization in exciting, long-
lasting and effective cross-cultural ministry
to kids and their leaders.

REACH A MILLION KIDS
Sponsor a needy international children's
outreach leader to reach kids for Christ in
their communities around the world.